T‌*CE*

"When my friend Carrie speaks—you lean in to listen. When she writes, you are drawn into every word narrating a beautiful story and bringing you into the moment. This book carries a vital message about the virtues, values, and moral character of our culture that are seemingly silent. Carrie invites us to restore the understanding and meaning of nobility, and I know it will unlock a generation to nobility, before it is too late."

Caitlin Zick, author of *Look at You, Girl* and codirector of Moral Revolution

"Nobility, so long associated with aristocracy, goes to the heart of what it is to be a graceful and loving Christian. In this superb book Carrie Lloyd lifts the veil from this forgotten word and we find we are looking at Jesus."

George Carey, former Archbishop of Canterbury (1991–2002), now Lord Carey

"Carrie's voice is a true treasure. She illuminates ideas and stories with her compassion, humor, and presence. *The Noble Renaissance* is a compelling work, gently moving us with a magnetic pull toward a deeper, more meaningful, Christ-centered life."

Amanda Lindsey Cook, singer-songwriter

"Society is hungry for personal growth, this we know. Books on how to change oneself are de rigueur these days, stocked up like pantry staples before a blackout—yet rarely do we find one that delves so deeply into a trait that, if attended to, can change every aspect of our lives. Carrie Lloyd, in *The Noble Renaissance*, has done exactly that. This incisive and steady journey deep into the applications and origins of nobility not only reveals treasure little, if ever, exposed to the light of day, but moves the heart toward actual transformation. Lloyd is both witty and kind—and in pursuing this attribute that she herself clearly prizes, she invites us all to a kind of life that is truly of another kingdom."

Teresa Archer, managing editor
for *Darling Magazine*

"In an increasingly chaotic and morally debased world, Carrie Lloyd taps into the inherent human drive to achieve a higher state of being and, by extension, a more noble relationship with other people and the world."

Michael Braverman, television executive producer

"In a cultural moment when doing what feels good in the moment is exalted, Carrie's prophetic battle cry has the power to awaken this generation and a sleeping church. With nuance, grace, and humility, Carrie invites us to live compelling lives of integrity, character, and compassion, and ultimately to reclaim the lost art of nobility in the everyday."

Katherine Harris, author, speaker, educator,
and host of *The Refined Collective Podcast*

THE
NOBLE
RENAISSANCE

RECLAIMING THE LOST VIRTUE OF NOBILITY

CARRIE LLOYD

EMANATE
BOOKS

Published in Nashville, Tennessee, by Emanate Books, an imprint of Thomas Nelson. Emanate Books and Thomas Nelson are registered trademarks of HarperCollins Christian Publishing, Inc.

Thomas Nelson titles may be purchased in bulk for educational, business, fund-raising, or sales promotional use. For information, please email SpecialMarkets@ThomasNelson.com.

Unless otherwise noted, Scripture quotations are taken from the New King James Version®. © 1982 by Thomas Nelson. Used by permission. All rights reserved.

Scripture quotations marked NLT are taken from the Holy Bible, New Living Translation. © 1996, 2004, 2007, 2013 by Tyndale House Foundation. Used by permission of Tyndale House Publishers, Inc., Carol Stream, Illinois 60188. All rights reserved.

Scripture quotations marked NASB are taken from the New American Standard Bible®, Copyright © 1960, 1962, 1963, 1968, 1971, 1972, 1973, 1975, 1977, 1995 by The Lockman Foundation. Used by permission. (www.Lockman.org)

Scripture quotations marked NIV are taken from the Holy Bible, New International Version®, NIV®. Copyright © 1973, 1978, 1984, 2011 by Biblica, Inc.® Used by permission of Zondervan. All rights reserved worldwide. www.Zondervan.com. The "NIV" and "New International Version" are trademarks registered in the United States Patent and Trademark Office by Biblica, Inc.®

Scripture quotations marked ESV are from the ESV® Bible (The Holy Bible, English Standard Version®). Copyright © 2001 by Crossway, a publishing ministry of Good News Publishers. Used by permission. All rights reserved.

Scripture quotations marked THE MESSAGE are from *The Message*. Copyright © by Eugene H. Peterson 1993, 1994, 1995, 1996, 2000, 2001, 2002. Used by permission of NavPress. All rights reserved. Represented by Tyndale House Publishers, Inc.

Scripture quotations marked KJV are from the King James Version. Public domain.

Any Internet addresses, phone numbers, or company or product information printed in this book are offered as a resource and are not intended in any way to be or to imply an endorsement by Thomas Nelson, nor does Thomas Nelson vouch for the existence, content, or services of these sites, phone numbers, companies, or products beyond the life of this book.

ISBN 978-0-7852-3175-2 (eBook)
ISBN 978-0-7852-3174-5 (TP)

Library of Congress Control Number: 2020933663

Printed in the United States of America
20 21 22 23 24 LSC 10 9 8 7 6 5 4 3 2 1

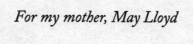

For my mother, May Lloyd

CONTENTS

FOREWORD

Nobility of character has never come through the laying on of hands with prayer or prophecy. It would be so much easier if it did. Character is instead built day-by-day, decision after decision, usually in the midst of conflict or challenging circumstances.

When we come to Christ, we become a new creation. We are given the mind of Christ, and the Holy Spirit comes to live inside of us, making our body His temple. His nature, the ultimate example of nobility, becomes our inheritance. But we make choices every day on whether we're going to align ourselves with what He has said or direct our hearts toward the inferior. Carrie Lloyd's *The Noble Renaissance* plants itself within the crossroads of those decisions. Her beautiful writing, filled with humor and her own vulnerability, urges all of us to pursue the noble life. When nobility becomes a priority, it has a profound effect on the world around us.

Character is never formed in the absence of options. For example, the Garden of Eden needed two trees: the Tree of the

Knowledge of Good and Evil and the Tree of Life. Adam and Eve had to have the chance to choose between what God said they were to do and what He said they were not to do. This choice was not given to them as some form of cruelty from God. Not hardly. Instead this was the God-given pathway for them to come into the fullness of all that He intended as they learned to accurately represent Him on earth. This was the entrance to His rewards, as there are no rewards where there are no options. Our loving heavenly Father is revealed as a father through rewarding the noble choices of His own. The strength of our role as co-laborers with Christ is solidified in our eagerness to choose well. This is the way of the noble.

The battle for nobility is wonderfully addressed in the parable of the seed and the sower found in Matthew 13. The seed in this story is the Word of God. Seeds carry possibilities that only the right environment can bring forth. The environment needed is good soil, water, and sunshine. But the same environment that causes the seed of God's Word over our lives to flourish also enables weeds to grow. The weeds are the words that are in conflict with what God has said. It's a strange picture in a sense, as God's Word is the most powerful thing in the universe. With it He created the worlds and brought transformation into our lives. Something as simple as a word that is in conflict with what God has said can become powerful but *only* when I give it my heart. I empower the weed to choke out the Word of God simply by giving it my attention. Thus, the choice for nobility is in the day to day. We must resolve not to give our hearts to the inferior, as nobility is found in our Christlike nature.

It is important that we learn to recognize the difference between what God has promised He would do for us and what He said He would do through us. In one case, He acts on our behalf. In the other, His promise is only fulfilled in our partnership, our nobility. But in the environment of the freedom He has established for us, we are able to allow other voices—anger, self-protection, fear—to take root in our lives in such a way that they choke out the Word of God. The Lord has allowed our choices to affect the most powerful thing in the universe as it pertains to our purpose and destiny. Choosing His Word over other options is the pathway to becoming noble.

The cry of *The Noble Renaissance* is for all of us to choose to follow the example Jesus became for us. Carrie delivers a powerful challenge, calling each of us to be intentional in our pursuit of the noble life. It's in the pursuit of nobility, she explains, that the people will see Christ within us. As Carrie writes, "[Jesus] displayed nobility with greater authority than anyone who crossed His path. Even unbelievers cannot disqualify the wisdom and teachings Jesus Christ personified." The world is hungry to experience the wisdom of heaven found in Jesus. But the manifestation of Jesus in our lives is entirely dependent on our surrender to the Word of God. It is time for a revival, not only of supernatural power, but also of purity, integrity, and nobility.

Author and friend Carrie Lloyd helps to fill a huge vacuum with this wonderful book on a subject that has almost been forgotten in most circles. I have had an unusual excitement anticipating the release of this book, almost like a child on Christmas morning ready to open gifts. *The Noble Renaissance* is just that for all of us: a wonderful gift that carries with it an invitation to beauty, to wonder, to nobility. I hope that you'll join with me and embrace the lifelong challenge to act with nobility when no one is watching so that we can be trusted with monumental decisions of influence when the nations are watching.

Bill Johnson
Bethel Church, Redding, California
Author of *When Heaven Invades
Earth* and *The Way of Life*

INTRODUCTION

It was found in Martin Luther King Jr.'s kneeling on Selma Bridge. It was witnessed in Rosa Park's rejection of the bus driver's order to relinquish her seat in the "colored section" to a white passenger after the whites-only section was filled. It was photographed when Father Alec Reid, a Catholic priest, read the last rites over the murdered bodies of two British corporals killed by the Provisional Irish Republican Army. It was conveyed in the breaking of bread with Judas. It housed orphans, rescued slaves, and forgave murderers. It caught the breath of the spectators when Pope Francis kissed a disfigured man in the crowds of the Vatican. Nobility does that.

It always catches the breath.

No matter your background, your creed, your race, or your preferences, the jaw-dropping, unique influence of the noble character is profound. Yet, is nobility—the father of virtues, once modeled so perfectly by Christ—in danger of being buried with bitterness, traditionalism, and the Amstrad computer? Are we instead becoming distracted with progressive liberalism, tribalistic kickbacks, failed attempts to rid the world of a Designer, and a penchant to become an art director on social media with our mother's flower arrangements?

In the current world of chaos, carnage, and cruelty, God knows we need to discover the art of nobility once more. We need to become noble in our own lives rather than waiting on the world to change.

I was heavily religious in my childhood. When I say religious, I mean the toe-curling, legalistic, can't-even-smile-at-an-emu approach to Christianity. (The Pharisees and I would have shared a wild glass of electrolyte water.) The type of religious that really would not have been able to gauge if Jesus had in fact left the building. Yes, the type that has created the current repulsion of the church by observers. My legalism had nothing to do with my parents' teachings, but had everything to do with my miscontextualization of Scripture and my lack of true intimacy with God. I made the journey from atheism in my twenties to become a devout Christian in my thirties. Through all these stages, I've walked through the valley, seen the shadow of death, shaken in fear at evil, but now have been graced with hopefully a deeper faith—some would say I found it by sheer chance. I would suggest it found me through the witness of noble men and women, people who truly walked out the gospel.

But, oh, how few there are. How few caught my breath.

I don't believe external persecution could ever kill Christianity. But I believe we, the very members of the body, could destroy any chance it has by our own lack of character and with our wishy-washy approach to the faith. Isaiah wrote that "a noble man devises noble plans; and by noble plans he stands" (32:8 NASB). Have we been doing that? Have we been planning at all? The telling signs of whether we believe we have renewed spirits are found in our character, how we respond to justice, to betrayal, to loss, to another's hurts.

From a legalistic, agenda-pushing, uncompassionate crusade of doctrine that we as a church intentionally or unintentionally created, we are now in the era of the backlash toward religion, the antiauthoritarian approach that then catalyzed a grace-led generation for the gospel. A component that perhaps the church needed. The grace-led gospel brought in again youthful numbers, but we became so focused on feelings, on niceties (let's face it, we all needed a hug by this point), and were so desperate for God's unconditional love for us that we concluded He just wanted us to be happy. And because of that, we discerned everything on the basis of our feelings. Not His feelings. Not His wisdom. Our ever-changing, unreliable, emotional roller-coaster nemesis. Cue the slow clap to this approach working out for us. We lost the line between what we felt the Spirit was telling us and our own dreams. Our discernment fell asleep, as did our wisdom.

In a time when we suffer the highest crime rates of identity theft the world has ever seen, so, too, there is an identity theft in the church right now. We believed the lie that told us Christ was just a bystander who occasionally helped you out in a tough spot—but not always. We forgot His teachings on sonship. Disappointment, loss, and betrayal set in, as they do on earth, not as it is in heaven; and we never learned how to endure tests with faith, with nobility. We weren't echoing His redemption, His restoration, His renewing of the mind. We found it hard to believe that Christ, in all of this, chose to reside in us. We kept knocking on doors around the world, hoping to find Him out there, when we never thought to cross our own thresholds— finding Him deep within our own souls.

In our pithy actions, we are not reflecting the abundance, the authority, the grace of the gospel. We're reflecting a limited, hopeless, weakened concept that rarely displays anything remotely like that of the apostles from the early church. It is as if such warriors have now become an anomaly.

In the pendulum swing of reacting to the world's revolt against religion, focusing too much on what the Enemy was doing, we lost the euphoric love of Jesus, what our Father was doing, the brutality of His love and the honest, sometimes painful, truth to His words. That although love is kind, and patient, it is also long-suffering, self-sacrificial, and downright gut-wrenchingly truthful. It is the salt and light (Matthew 5:13–16). Never relying on the praises of the world or acquiescing to its customs.

It is noble.

Nobility is a beautiful amalgam of many virtues that this book plans to unpack. I intend to lay them out before you, with a hope that the mind, body, and spirit might be inspired once more to come back to basic truths: the power of character, its steadfastness when built and developed over time. The cultures we can change, the justice we can promote, the revival we could finally steward, if only we lived by a noble character instead of following a subjective heart.

Within our own brokenness as a church, we cannot hide from the rest of the earth. We must help and aid the world back to greater wisdom. To the brutally simple gospel of love, light, and liberty. True liberty. Not the shackled concepts the secular world believes we need today. We must be set apart from the world so that we can bring hope, comfort, and life to its max capacity.

If Christians are to stand for anything anymore, it is not in the perfectionism of religion or the judgment of legalism. It must be found in the morality of our character and the excellence of spirit that could tear down the Goliaths. It could have faith for a wiser tomorrow, could heal the sick with a shadow, could heal the blind with lashings of mud, could perforate division with courageous acts of unreasonable kindness, could introduce anyone back to their real identity—the one that was formed in the all-loving, all-glowing goodness of God. You'd not just have a bunch of believers roaming the earth; you'd have a crusade of lovers, crashing into every dilemma with solutions at their restorative fingertips, because they stopped for a moment and asked themselves, *Who am I really? Why are we here?* And in all matters: *What's the noble choice?*

In observing the world at such a crucial tie in history, my questions for all of us are:

Will you stand when the kingdom needs you to make the honest, the bloody, the terrifying, the courageous, the bolder moves of integrity, of truth? Will you understand that there is no narcotic strong enough to match the sensations that a noble choice makes? For the soul only likes to sing along to the steadfast and victorious harmonies of heaven. We were wired for goodness. We were geared for family, for the Father's embrace, for love.

Today, whether the battle you face to display nobility is a fully fledged militant one or an encounter with a cantankerous bus driver, sleep upon the hope that the struggle delights our Lord more than the temporary comfort of an easier route.

For one posture breathes eternity; the other lasts no longer than a carton of juice.

NOBILITY

For centuries we reverted to nobility
as a place for the elite, a home for the
aristocracy, but never did we consider it an
option open to us, the everyday man.

Not until now.

CHAPTER 1

BAREFOOT IN THE RAIN

WHAT IS NOBILITY?

She was at a breaking point. A black hoodie covered her head as she stood next to a pay phone in the bucketing rain. Broken flip flops and soaked-through socks adorned her feet.

Most people would have walked on, preferring to watch a viral video on their smartphones of a man rescuing a baby deer out of a swimming pool.

If they had noticed our heroine with no quarter to her name, they might have had a few different responses:

- Do nothing at all. It was her choice to live like this.
- Ask if she is okay. If there is no response, we did our part, the ball had now indubitably been placed in her court.

But Callie, a twenty-three-year-old passerby, took a third option. She felt a nudge that only the selfless can feel—the nudge to persevere and strike up a conversation.

This lass was a tough audience. Callie felt bolted to the ground, compelled to stay and undo the disconnection between them one question at a time. The young woman's story was unique, as it is with every homeless individual: a recently deceased father, a burned-down house, an abusive boyfriend. Between her explanations they stared at each other, a silent dialogue of observations between the pauper and the princess, and Callie didn't like it.

"What's your shoe size?" Callie asked.

"A woman should never ask a lady what her shoe size is!"

"Oh, I'm sorry," Callie replied, wiping rain from her face. "I didn't know that."

An awkward silence was followed by a hopeless whisper. "*Size nine.*"

A breakthrough.

Callie took off her sneakers, grieved a little in her spirit, inwardly saying, *Goodbye, little friends—you have been kind to me,* and handed over her favorite pair of shoes. (Size nine, in case you were nervous to ask.)

"I'm embarrassed to take these," the women sputtered.

"Why? When this is a privilege for me to care for you in this moment?" Callie replied with a smile.

The young woman opened her hands to receive them and was persuaded to retreat into the gas station. These were the cashier's two new guests: barefoot Callie and the lady in the rain, holding not just her flip-flops but now also a pair of Adidas. She was still unsure whether to actually wear them. Callie grabbed other supplies for her new friend.

"Can I pray for you?"

A pregnant pause. They both were aware they had an audience. As you can imagine, it was quite a spectacle for those in the gas station. Callie had now built a new church in the middle of this food mart. The woman replied, "Yes. Well, er, yes. I mean . . . yes." Still holding the shoes, she took down her hoodie.

"I really feel Jesus has a massive story for your life," Callie said.

"Well, He must have a big sense of humor because this isn't how I'd write the story line."

"I understand. But it's about to get really good."

These are the moments of *active* love I long for: so extravagant, so untimely—shaking up our own agendas—so scripted by God, hoping that we will come out and play our part. So often we miss them. And this extravagance is not in terms of wealth necessarily but made up of choices that result in sometimes undignified, sometimes inconvenient, costs for us.

The woman opened her eyes to a sensation of warmth throughout her entire body, a familiar description when people meet the Holy Spirit for the first time. This woman never asked for Callie's name. Too focused on her own pain, she was in no position to help others. And this millennial (Callie) didn't carry out the gesture to then post it on Instagram or to wait for even an ounce of gratitude. This moment was necessary for someone to go above, to be set apart for this moment and introduce her to an uncommon kindness.

"Hey. Where did the chick go?"

She couldn't find Callie anywhere. Putting on her new Adidas, she looked around the food mart.

"She left once she knew you were going to be all right," the cashier replied.

Searching for Angel Adidas, the woman looked through the window, and across the court was Callie, walking away into the night.

Barefoot in the rain.

It's here, right here, where something more holy than just being a "good person" takes place. Where a divine wisdom longs to encounter the lost, the broken, the rejected, and He is seeking the tenderhearted to execute it (2 Chronicles 34:27).

The *good* might make space for such gestures in their calendars; the *noble* will interrupt their schedules. The *good* might pass on some money; the *noble* give up their prized possessions. The *good* might think it's best to give "tough love" in the situation (to give money would enable their poor choices); the *noble* ask questions, never assuming that just because they've seen this before, the reason is the same.

Nobility resides in the difference between random acts of kindness and standards of moral codes that go beyond the expected, the rational, the norm. Forgiving the unforgivable, showing kindness toward the offensive, or, like Jesus, washing the feet of the one who is calculating your death.

It's the distinction between Christians who say they believe and Christians who truly walk out the gospel.

It is, in the words of A. W. Tozer, "the excellence of moral beings."[1]

And I fear that if we are not careful, we will lose the virtue altogether. When was the last time you heard anyone mention the word *noble*? It's important to distinguish what *noble* means, and why we should place our hope in it once more.

The word *noble* comes with a few definitions. It could be considered the rank of a distinguished status, persons belonging to hereditary class (the aristocracy).

OR:

It is a person of exalted moral character.

We'll be looking at the latter, the same definition I believe encompasses the very nature of Christ—the most perfect person who ever breathed. He displayed nobility with a greater authority than anyone who crossed His path. Even unbelievers cannot disqualify the wisdom and teachings Jesus Christ personified. And they cannot ignore the power of His influence, despite the fact that He neither owned nor ruled anything. For the believer He is the Son of God, the sinner's Savior, the Redeemer, the Healer, the incarnation of perfection. For the unbeliever He is still one of the world's greatest thinkers.

So wherever you stand, His teachings on good character, on wise responses, could be administered by anyone, and still they would find dramatic results. Of course, if you have found salvation, this is merely the beginning, not the end, of your journey in the Christian faith. It's often the lack of nobility in the Christian faith that makes me question a few things.

Exalted or moral character comes with many strands of virtue, and nobility is the umbrella that covers them all. Let's journey together to dissect those virtues, thread by thread, in a manner that will make each one of us want to put *nobility* back in our vocabulary.

When Michael Hart listed the top one hundred most influential people in the world, I was rather stunned to see that Jesus was ranked at number three.

Muhammad was placed first.

Isaac Newton ranked at number two.[2]

I mentally weighed the attributes of both parties:

Newton discovered gravity.

Jesus Christ is the Son of God, the same God who created Newton.

Newton invented the first reflective telescope.

Jesus, a carpenter, probably made a nice set of nesting tables at one point, but was also a prolific and radical thinker. Two thousand years later, 2.19 billion people believe and follow the practices of His teachings.

Or do they?

When asked why Christ wasn't ranked at number one, Hart suggested he would have easily handed Christ the number one position, if only His followers had actually carried out the teachings He gave us.[3]

A highly distinctive viewpoint is presented in Matthew 5:43–44:

"Ye have heard that it hath been said, Thou shalt love thy neighbor, and hate thine enemy. But I say unto you, Love your enemies, bless them that curse you, do good to them that hate you, and pray for them which despitefully use you, and persecute you."

And a few lines earlier: "resist not evil, but whosoever shall smite thee on the right cheek, turn to him the other also." Now, these ideas—which were not a part of the Judaism of Jesus' day, nor of most other religions—are surely among the most remarkable and original ethical ideas ever presented. If they were widely followed, I would have had no hesitation in placing Jesus first in this book.

But the truth is that they are not widely followed. In fact, they are not even generally accepted.[4]

I wish I had evidence to prove Hart wrong. Today, we (the church) are not famous for loving the hell out of people, as Christ did. We are not known to be the peacemakers, as Christ was. We have not welcomed all sinners to our table, as Christ would. And don't get me started on how we interact on Instagram when one Christian has a different theology than another. We're about as poised as Helga Pataki from television's *Hey Arnold!*

To much of the world, we as a body have been guilty of covering up sexual abuse cases, picketing outside soldiers' funerals, red-taping our mouths outside abortion clinics instead of sitting and talking with the women entering. *Forget sitting at Jacob's well; we've got eye-catching banners!* We have inspired people with fascinating theologies, but how many of us are truly carrying them out? Regularly, day to day, minute to minute? Acts of nobility are pointedly included throughout the Bible. There are too many moments to count that record Bible characters' actions of sacrifice, their integrity, their noble choices.

Are we truly set apart? Are we truly emulating God's glory in our everyday actions? Or are we just getting by as a matter of survival, a matter of salvation? Have we lost the intention of noble gestures completely? Did we ever place that word into our vocabulary?

I'm not sure I did.

About a year ago, in my newfound obsession with this concept, I posed the question to friends on Facebook: "If I say the word *noble*, who comes to mind?" I received the following expected responses:

William Wilberforce

Martin Luther King Jr.

Mother Teresa

Florence Nightingale

Corrie ten Boom

Gandhi

Jesus

Man alive, I was so glad Christ finally came into the mix!

Household names and history makers took precedence in the answers, but not one answer named a friend or someone they might know personally, as if the traits of noble character were unobtainable if you weren't born into the right family. The noble were unreachable and rare. Perhaps nobility was an inherited personality trait handed down the family line that only the very privileged could discover. Like being a monarch. Such breeding is a divine appointment. Only so many can sit on the throne. These were the big guns. I wondered, what if we developed a belief that nobility was a gift, rather than a choice? If it was an anointing, instead of a muscle intentionally built and developed over time. Or a kind reward handed over like knighthood.

It's not something you are—it's something you have.

I could see why nobility was a lost art form, when these icons were the standard set before us. A mountainous feat that seemed like too much work.

But if we take those names above and feast on their biographies, hardships, conquests, and despairing roots to courageous overcoming, we see they were everyday people at some point, making choices just like the rest of us. They, too, felt the pangs of heartbreak; they, too, had to decide what flavor marmalade to put on their whole-grain toast.

In watching the small, everyday choices of people I considered worthy of being called noble, I realized nobility is just like water. It's available to everyone. Perhaps we just haven't had nobility modeled for us. Maybe we never considered it even as an option in our everyday lives. It needn't be left for those social justice speeches by President Reagan, "Mr. Gorbachev, tear down this wall!" Rather, it is in choosing the right path in the mundane dilemmas: overcharging a client, retaliation against those unkind tweets, bitterness toward an ex, a frustrating phone call with customer service, succumbing to the pretty secretary who thinks you hung the moon when the wife at home is never satisfied, refusing to let the car jump in front of you because they skipped the line of traffic—leading to our anger blowing up in a soundproofed rage.

Every hour we have options. I'm not sure we have realized yet how powerful we could be—not only for ourselves but for our Lord—if we took ownership of our own characters and their development. This isn't a make-do attitude or striving for perfection. It's a stretch that functions from a spirit of adoption. A "like Father, like son" approach that lets heaven have a stronger presence in the smallest of moments. For that is where character is built. It rides on a purpose far greater than our own disgruntlement.

Such poise is threaded like silk throughout the Scripture. In people like Daniel, like Joseph, like Paul. Their integral moves created prolific story lines, documented for us to learn from, to dote upon.

Within these nobles are similarities, elements in character necessary for noble people to rise, take shape, and shift cultures, movements even, one action at a time. The elements of nobility, if nurtured and developed well, could indeed make the most unlikely of candidates a historic world changer. I doubt they set up their lives to be so impactful, for their humility didn't seek the spotlight, but their paths turned out to be poignant.

Nobility can be broken down into components, and each component cannot live without the other. Like the circle of life, they have to feed and rejuvenate to keep each other alive. You cannot be generous if you cannot be self-sacrificial. You cannot be honorable without humility. You cannot be diligent without courage. You cannot persevere without integrity.

Self-sacrifice, humility, perseverance, honor in justice, wisdom, courage, and integrity all ride on the carousel of nobility. At least that's what I've been told in my dreams, what I've observed in the Scriptures. How we manage pain also helps or hinders our noble acts. And if you look closer, the virtues are the nemesis to the seven deadly sins:

Envy—Integrity
Gluttony—Processing pain
Greed—Self-sacrifice
Lust—Wisdom
Pride—Humility
Sloth—Perseverance
Wrath—Honor in justice (compassion)

A NOTE TO THE READER

To avoid misplaced assumptions, I'm going to make a confession. This may come as a shock to you, so be sure to be sitting down.

I am not noble.

But I'm trying to be.

It's going to take some time. I write not as a victor who has conquered the subject, but as a student, inspired, hoping the more I teach the more it will rub off on my own personal choices. I can already propose that even using the word on our lips again, even mentioning it in dialogue, can make a difference. I have noticed with the pastors I work with and the students I guide, we are facing the same adversities with different strategies. But whenever we posture our hearts right in adversity, we always win.

Hard to believe. But it's true. At least it's true when it comes to the kingdom of God. Death may have taken Stephen's life, the first martyr of the early church, but to be brutally honest with you, I don't think he even noticed (Acts 7:54–60). Caught up with Christ standing up for him in the cloud of witnesses above, he sort of didn't see the whole "execution" thing. Besides, it was just for a mere moment. Death is really just a speed bump away from heaven.

I truly believe that the nobles look upon the world with a kingdom perspective so uniquely different from the rest of us, it's as if they were supernatural beings that focus on the outcomes, instead of on thunderous internal and external threats.

Today

The early church was built on a few things, two of which were virtues and power. We often like to look at power and hosting God's presence, but are we truly reverent when it comes to extraordinary acts that not only reflect our virtues but counteract the expectations of modern culture?

We are watching the generation that says 56 percent of Gen-Yers won't work at a company if it bans social-media access; more than half aren't willing to cave in to requests at work for the sake of their own digital hobbies. And yet, "84 percent of the same generation believe that helping to make a positive difference in the world is more important than professional recognition."[5] We're willing to make a difference when it doesn't cost us anything, but are we when we need to lay something down?

The millennials are arguably the most charitable generation and yet the most self-focused. We'll give money, but won't perhaps give our time. Much like a difficult relationship, perseverance is trumped by wanting to make an impact. Patience is bulldozed by the instant gratification of the digital era. An online influencer was paid $250,000 to put one tile on Instagram for a music festival that was an economic disaster.[6] The tireless locals who worked thousands of hours building the venue for the event were left with nothing, penniless and exhausted.

It's a world of double standards: vengeful justice without taking ownership, toxic disagreements on freedom of speech, yet there is a Christian genocide erupting as I write. Ethical grass-fed burgers are more requested by the youth than any other generation, yet adolescents are clicking on porn more than ever. People have more intimacy with their smartphones than with actual people. We are the most liberated society the world has ever seen, but anxiety and depression is at its all-time highest.

With pills, therapy, and self-help books, we become quite focused on ourselves and our own healing journeys. Which is important, but it can't be the whole story or the entire life plan. This is where Christianity comes in, or should come in. Delivering the gospel is not the headcount at the altar for those being saved; it's in the making of disciples. It's transformation in individual lifestyles that transforms the family, that transforms the workplace, that transforms cities, that transforms the world.

Of North American metroplexes, Dallas, Texas, has the greatest density of Christians in its geographic sphere. Christians might believe that the more Christians there are in a given demographic, the better off the city will be. But Dallas's social statistics—the high figures of crime and violence, economic decline, decrepit social systems, oppression of women, racial division—prove an opposite statement. We've become content with salvation instead of the true mandate to look beyond the church. I'm beginning to believe that our echoes of the gospel aren't enough to make more of the world believe in the Bible. The gospel needs to be reflected by individuals and their noble deeds, by every opportunity we have to display not just power but integrity, mercy, and kindness.

There are persons who roam the earth looking out for others, laying down their lives for others, giving to others, quieting the distress of others, rescuing others, pouring into a fresh legacy. And I hope it will be these people who corrupt the chaos of this self-focused evolution.

Occasionally, though, we do hear stories that make it through the weedy manipulations of the Internet. With tales as old as time, parables are loaded with the good news in disguise. Through YouTube viral videos, we are invited to remember what really makes us come alive. The virtues that are often only referred to these days in eulogies at funerals. Especially if we are looking at the world as one unit.

And there are thousands of these stories: the man who donated two hundred thousand air miles to strangers so they could go home to their families for Christmas. The Buffalo fire-fighters who carried a man ten blocks to Mercy Hospital (note the name) because the ambulance saving this man from a heart attack got stuck in a blizzard. The family who welcomed a deaf baby into the world and discovered that twenty of their neighbors learned sign language before the baby's arrival. A teenager who saved up for two years to buy his friend a wheelchair.

And, arguably, who wouldn't save a baby deer from a swimming pool? On many occasions we have instinctive responses toward doing good, but then there are the out-of-the-way, gut-wrenching choices that will cost us, sometimes our lives. That's nobility: the choice to do something we don't have to do, but something greater than us that urges us to push beyond our capacity.

If eternity is set in the heart of man (Ecclesiastes 3:11), it can certainly show in the most chaotic, most adverse circumstances. We assist in making all things good by making noble choices in co-laboring with God. In our personal response to chaos or darkness, we get to reflect eternity outward to the secular world.

When I began to ask the questions, *What's the noble choice? What would Jesus do?* I noted how different my approach to any situation became. Whether I acted on the noble choice is another question. I often took the easier road. The cop-out. The avoidance. The choice to forgive but keep them at arm's length and not answer their calls, so help me God. *Oh, but how I wish them well!* I'd tell myself. I wasn't noble. I am still perhaps not that noble. But with this new awakening, I hope to bring my friends with me. I've never been good at doing things alone.

I'm learning through observations, through research, through personal trial and error, that this virtue is the godfather of the virtues.

We all need to stop using excuses; we all need to face the pain and choose the harder path of nobility over the easier path of comfort or, worse yet, of denial.

Why? Why do we need it? Why add another item onto the to-do list of those who reside in "squeaky-clean Christianville"?

Because seeking nobility is one of the most healing encounters I've ever experienced. It's love in its purest form. Because what we have tried to manipulate and control with our actions doesn't really work. The choices don't bring peace; they bring heartbreak. And I'm tired of division. Of the raging worlds that fill up broadcasting—of what used to be good solid information.

In the name of justice, we've robbed ourselves of noble aptitudes. In the name of our own needs being met, we put Jesus at number three. In the name of opinion, we've lost how to love amid the propaganda. In the name of success, of influencing the influential, we've left the moneyless alone with a pay phone.

But when I learn of stories I so wish to share with you, names unknown and known, there is a bowing down to such people. The humblest, ironically, will find people naturally bend to them, as if they were born into some sort of command.

If you're anything like me, and you're starved for noble stories of heart-wrenching kindness that hits the soul more times than a piñata, well, they are out there. The trait of nobility is obtainable. We just need to learn the elements, the ways of the wise.

After all, I'm tired of walking comfortably. I think God's glory deserves a little more than this.

Who knows? The road to nobility could start with one divine appointment, one encounter with Jesus, that leaves you walking without your Adidas, barefoot in the rain.

FOR SELF-REFLECTION

The noble are everyday people. What is holding you back from believing you could be noble too?

Begin to ask "What's the noble choice?" in your everyday encounters and decisions. What differences do you discern?

The lack of nobility has made some people question the influence Jesus had on the planet. But Jesus is the embodiment of nobility. Are there stories of His life that you can relate to in this theme?

Nobility is made up of different elements: integrity, processing pain, perseverance, humility, self-sacrifice, courage, wisdom, and how we respond to justice. Where do you excel? And where do you struggle?

Nobility is the invitation to fully live out the very thing Christ died for: our new man. The new us. Write a vision of yourself now that the old man has died. What do you look like? How do you react?

Nobility is not something to be expected overnight; it is a constant conversation to last the rest of our lives. What practices can you place in your life that will give you enough self-compassion to let the search for nobility be a journey rather than a goal?

THE BEGINNINGS OF NOBILITY: RIGHTEOUSNESS

Threaded in the disappointments of our
journey is the choice to persevere with
kindness or grow in wrath or bitterness.
The former invites more discoveries
of the mysteries of God; the latter
merely highlights the darker parts of a
character that is refusing to change.

CHAPTER 2

PASS THE MILK

RIGHTEOUSNESS

ow would Mrs. Thatcher like to go all day without a drink? I voted conservative but that's finished! It's finished now you've cut milk for the children. Hurting children is absolutely the end. Little children need a drink, is it fair? In this day and age, is it fair?!"[1]

It was 1971, and England's education secretary was under fire. Headlines such as "Thatcher, Thatcher the Milk Snatcher" and "Thatcher Caned for School Milk" weren't helping.

The seventies in Britain had become the modern-day Dark Ages: trade union stoppages, ethnic tensions, and miners' strikes placing major thoroughfares, shops, and restaurants in darkness for days. Even television was cut short for several nights. Alongside classism, football fans (or soccer, to Americans) kept battering their wives as a cathartic outlet for disappointing game results. Literature was producing uplifting titles such as *Is Britain*

Dying? and polarization of politics was at its worst. Something people both in the UK and the US might relate to.

But when the education secretary, Margaret Thatcher, cut costs for the national budget by removing free milk in school from children ages seven to eleven (children under the age of seven or any child feeling ill could still have milk for free all week), well, now we were really mad. Margaret Thatcher was one hour away from personal effigies filling up Parliament, and the prime minister even considered firing her. It was her gender that saved her from the sack; they couldn't possibly be the party to fire the only female MP in cabinet. Members of the House of Commons brawled and chanted names, "Attila the Hun" being an all-round favorite. Some of the public accused her of trying to reintroduce rickets to the poorer classes of children by removing milk. She was hurt, shocked, and had been unaware that removing a few items from the school expenditure, saving the government from going into debt, would amount to sheer bedlam.

Television crews interviewed sorrowful children. "What do you think of no longer getting free milk at school?" one reporter asked.

"It's not fair," a boy replied.

"Why not?"

"Because I like it."

It was a different, veganless time.

But the response to injustice hasn't changed. We overreact, battle the wrong things, cause the wrong people pain, or discard people altogether.

How we respond to injustice, even if it is over milk, is what distinguishes the noble from the ignoble. The righteous from the hyper-offendable. The merciful from the entitled. Kind intentions from the downright appalling. The wise from the foolish. The greater the injustice, the greater the opportunity to let heaven invade earth; but how often do we witness truly great character in the face of the hate? Not as often as I would hope.

This is where Christ shone brightest. Within the stench of true injustice and inequality, His wisdom left crowds silent, whether in awe or rage. How dare He heal on the Sabbath or talk to the Samaritans? He had a way that ricocheted off the ignorant and religious but would change the course of our mortal lives forever. For there has been no greater injustice than the crucifixion of the most perfect One. And we all know how that turned out.

Noble actions have crucified evil injustices, but it took radical methods to oppose cruelty and prejudice. The civil rights movement of India rooted itself in a nonviolent approach. The movement was an outstanding example, one that not only propelled a wave of compassion from the entire world, but one that challenged the current law of its day. Activists prayed not only for freedom but for the freedom of the oppressor. This model of "passive action" was administered by Mahatma Gandhi, the man who almost singlehandedly brought independence to India. A man who, before joining the independence party for India, experienced racist tension first in South Africa, where he also made friends with Christians, and where he gained some foundational learnings for his calling to come. My friend Robert Van De Weyer, a lay preacher and philosopher from Cambridge who worked for the Gandhi organization in India, told me something amazing: "He [Gandhi] always said the two documents that meant the most to him were the Sermon on the Mount and the Bhagavad Gita. . . ."

Christ's most famous sermon—the moral teachings of mercy, the beatitudes, the salt and light manifesto—inspired and led one man to break India free from the racist oppressions of the British Empire 1,915 years later.

A former barrister who studied in England, Gandhi faced abhorrent segregation and classism. After he made his home once again in India, he asked all Indian citizens, despite the racial beatings and violent attacks, to never, ever, fight back. Amid their silent protests, massacres bloodied the stone pavements. These killings—including mothers and children—were led by threatened and power-hungry British troops. Rioting by the Hindus and Muslims justified the British Empire even more. Gandhi believed that he who acted with the higher nobility, one who stood his cause but never fought back with vengeance or violence, would inspire his enemies so much that they would one day lay down their weapons. And if the Indians did stoop as low, raging an eye for an eye, Gandhi would take the blow upon himself, refusing food, fasting until there was silence.

The noble are willing to die in righteousness rather than live by vengeful means.

More and more Christians from England were enamored by Gandhi's approach. Oh, the irony that a Hindu was inspiring, even introducing Christians to their own doctrine: "I tell you not to resist an evil person. But whoever slaps you on your right cheek, turn the other to him also" (Matthew 5:39). Often, we as a church have not responded with nonviolence (both physically and verbally), with patience, with questions, with an open dialogue.

Justice is not passive; it does not ignore the oppressor. It stands its ground, but rarely with anger and never with throwdowns. It's creative. It's dignified. It doesn't sucker-punch the culprit but takes the suffering itself. This is the beautiful part of Jesus' third way: it suffers so that another generation doesn't have to. It is creative, clever, but never cruel.

We may think that power and influence will bring justice, that power can only be derived from a greater power. Or apparently a good slap on the face will bring reconciliation. That witty quips and cutting opinions will redeem. That only by suffocation of the other's voice can justice win. Why else is there so much arguing online? Why else do we see so many Christians defame, downgrade, and butcher others' opinions?

We wonder why our children are leaving the faith, why they don't respect their parents' words, why our numbers are plummeting. But modeling noble character teaches concepts that words never can. We listen to someone who is kind more than to an orator who is coldhearted. The children have been watching the fruit of our actions. I did not leave the church during my twenties because of disbelief in Christ; I left the church because it responded terribly to sinners. And I, believe it or not, was often one of those who responded poorly. I wasn't gaining insight into why I was carrying out acts I did, why I behaved in a way that wasn't helpful. Instead the judgment stayed standing, without explanation or a nursing hand.

Sin leads to its own death. And when it comes to injustices, we seek the people who caused them or point to God. Rarely is there trust in a mighty God who wants the very best for us. Even insurance companies blame acts of nature on God. And due to this lack of trust, we take things into our own hands. Be it trolls or vigilantes, people take the law, the rules, religion, a wrathful gospel into their own hands, with their own methods. As if it's their job—even their right—to dictate another's destiny. The ignoble react in their pain and in their hurt. But when the noble face injustice, they act with courage and are filled with patience, long-suffering, and peace. They stand mighty. Alone. Nobility holds an honor that is breathtaking and heart-wrenching all in one poetic gesture. When the noble trust in a power much mightier than themselves, they do only what they can do, leaving the perpetrator to their own devices (unless many others are being hurt, as was the case in India). Then it takes only one noble soul, holding neither power nor Twitter clout, to begin the momentum to change history.

The beautiful lesson within the story of Mahatma Gandhi's activism was observing his lack of qualification. He had no influence in the military, no Pulitzer prize, no stake in wealth or land. No scientific mind, no artistic achievement could have made the impact this man had on an entire nation. Instead, his passion for freedom, his bravery to speak the truth with gentle confrontation, his heart for humility over power freed a country from the oppressive grips of the British Empire.

Albert Einstein said (about Gandhi), "Generations to come, it may be, will scarce believe that such a one as this ever, in flesh and blood, walked upon this earth."

Martin Luther King Jr.'s civil rights movement, William Wilberforce's crusade for the abolition of the slave trade, Emmeline Pankhurst's suffragette campaign, Malala Yousafzai's protest against the Taliban's prejudice against women, all proved that no one has to be in power to find redemption, and manipulation never wins authority; it merely repels it.

We might think we have no need to stand up and engage in this kind of discourse. India is still free. Most Western civilians are not living in oppressive conditions that warrant such intense response. Women can vote. The Taliban are finding it harder to murder innocents by plane thanks to our security regulations. And the Anglican church has finally allowed female bishops. So what's my point?

We're still fighting. Over racism, over poor conduct, over prejudicial behavior, over unequal rights and unequal treatment of genders. There are still injustices going on. But we're also fighting over stupid things. Where the truly ignoble rise to the surface.

And I mean the most ridiculous arguments. I've been privy to a few myself, overhearing all manner of fights. Does one leave the toilet paper over or under? Does turning up the air conditioning make it hotter or colder? Who stunted the growth of the broccoli in the back garden? The correct pronunciation of the word *selfish*—a loud, challenging row in the middle of quiet coach D on the ten o'clock train to St. Pancras.

Human fetal tissue is being trafficked for profit, but arguments about the stunted growth of broccoli, of milk, of a preacher being flown by a friend's jet—this is where we get really passionate.

The noble choose to fight the right fights; their compassion takes over the need to let the ego ride on the high of discourse. It also refuses to enjoy getting scared, getting caught up in the fearmongering so much of the press profits from today.

Murder is a brutal sin; just like our approach to the price of fuel, we are all in agreement on that one. But a fair few of us seem to forget the power of the tongue, that words poised for emotional harassment and verbal attack are as toxic to the soul as violence is to the body. Sticks and stones do break the bones, and words do hurt you; words poison the spirit. Death or life—your choice. I know, it's a strong stance.

When the Samaritan woman fetched water from Jacob's well, she was visiting it in the hottest part of the day, unlike the other women who came to the well in the earlier, cooler hours (John 4). She also existed in a time when there had been a century-long feud between the Jews and the Samaritans. She was oppressed, criticized, judged, and hated. When we meet her in the book of John, we're already aware she's an outcast. Not only that, but the most prolific teachings in the Jewish culture, the Mishnah, make it clear how to handle Samaritan women—don't talk with them and don't share spittle with them, a carnal sin, one as foul as eating swine. So when Christ asked her for a swig of water, He was asking to use her watering can or camel pouch. This wasn't a compliment to her; this was an insult. She took a shot at Christ, figuratively speaking: "Are you greater than our father Jacob, who gave us the well and drank from it himself, as did also his sons and his livestock?" (v. 12 NIV). Her feathers are unequivocally ruffled, in her sense of insecurity as a Samaritan, and like most people feeling wrongly rebuked by age-old prejudice, she's edgier than a Transformer.

Just as it happens today, most of society pronounced judgment on her. They heard some distant rumor of five husbands and the cohabitant she wasn't even married to. They labeled her—the adulterer, the sinful one—and cast her out into the ether of nowhere-land. They bracketed her and placed her outside the community. Words ostracize just as much as leprosy isolates you from the crowd.

It's repugnant, but you only need to open the newspaper to see how quickly we do that today. The church included. We despise a certain theology. We hatch plans to walk out of a pastor's sermon if we disapprove of their choice for president. True story. We dishonor, even if it just be the withholding of love. Half of England apparently doesn't like Meghan Markle. Perhaps as much as 99.5 percent of Englanders have never spoken to her. Perhaps we make judgments and cases for "just" arguments, within our own limited fears. Perhaps there's some unhealthy delight in forming hate groups riddled with nonsense. Do we like the comradery? There's fellowship in Christ, and then there's fellowship in toxic thoughts. Do we know the difference? We create these fears through our own lenses, our personal experiences, codings formed with our upbringing, which then lead to assumptions and doctrines that rest outside of the all-merciful gospel. In short, we're often full of justice when nothing carnally unjust has actually happened.

Returning to the outcast, the oppressed, the rejected, what exactly did this Samaritan woman do to society, other than hurt herself with a bad catalogue of men? Did anyone even ask? Divorce at that point could not be initiated by women. After all, they were considered unreliable, untrustworthy sources in a court of law. She didn't run through five men; five men (potentially) ran through her. For if it had anything to do with the more liberal side of the law and the Hallel teachings, men could have divorced her for burning the toast. But Jesus saw the outcast and asked questions— questions to determine if she was able to tell her own truths. How encouraged Christ was to see that she was not in denial, nor did she justify her situation. She told it like it was. It's only in truth that we can ever find breakthrough. It's within truth that justice is served.

And despite her edgy rebuttals, Jesus ploughed on in the dialogue, ignoring her comments, to administer the real understanding of His justice, "to lift up" another, to tell her what the real problem was. Just as He was lifted up upon the cross, as He was lifted up into glory at the time of His ascension, so did He see justice as a lifting up of others. Joseph, His earthly father, had a similar approach. It couldn't have been easy on the heart strings to know your fiancée was pregnant when you played no part. The sentence for any betrothed women who had lain with another man during engagement was death. But Joseph, called a "just man," sought to quietly divorce her (Matthew 1:19). We see all Jesus' decision making as what His Father was doing, but His earthly father modeled a beautiful rendition of a heavenly justice while Jesus was being birthed into this world. Yes, Joseph was comforted after an angel's visit, but before then, he could have retaliated, reacted (as most do) in pain and anger, suffering the regret and consequences of the conscience later.

Jesus sought the true reason the Samaritan woman was suffering—a lack of satisfaction under huge amounts of oppression, of rejection. He didn't label her, He didn't reject her because of her choices, He didn't call her out to punish her sin. He lifted her up, giving her a real answer to the *real* problem, and in the lifting up He cleansed away the shame.

That's true justice.

A justice for *all*.

Too many people seek out those who create injustice and form campaigns to obliterate, to curtail the power of the unjust, as if the punishment will fit the crime. But that's only in a court of law; it doesn't fly in the court of Christ's kingdom. I agree with freedom for all, I agree with equality, and I believe in Martin Luther King Jr.'s dream. But this third approach for justice is being forgotten today.

A plethora of people are trying to be twenty-five feet tall behind a ten-inch screen. The Internet has created a medium for unrestrained opinions to let loose. The power of the pen, the written word, has become as virile as prejudice itself, but because some people believe they are fighting to defend God's doctrine, or just their own understanding of what is right, they seem to ignore God's position on justice. We are not called to defend God; we are called to emulate Him.

The noble emulate Him.

The #MeToo movement is a power play by today's females. But the allowance of the power plays, the sexual dalliances, and the uplifting of power instead of people is exactly what got us into this mess. So we got the Harvey Weinsteins into jail, we smeared many people's reputations in the press, and we celebrated that their wives left them. I'm not sure heaven is cheering though. The truth always comes into the light, yes, but I'm pretty certain we left out the mercy, the humility, the love part of the equation. Does placing sex addicts behind bars really solve the problem? Perhaps for a week. For a year. But the greater justice would have been rehabilitation for the men too.

Today's world does not provide a safe environment for wrong-doers to surrender, to apologize, to white-flag their way out. It's not a warm environment in which to admit our faults, our struggles, our pain. The guilty might want to come out, admit defeat, and jump into a field of truth and freedom, but when they do take a look outside, they see nothing but a pit of vipers. Some

Christians don't confess because they see how the church has cast out or humiliated sinners, and the cost is too great. Homosexuals dare not come to church because we've handled sexual issues with no kindness, no conversation, no open questions.

"Act justly . . . love mercy . . . walk humbly" (Micah 6:8 NIV).

I long for the day when someone calls me about sexual harassment I endured two decades ago. I long for those calls, not to vilify the perpetrators, not to shame them into jail, but for the opportunity to reply to the reporters: "But I already spoke with him about this the week after it happened. Sixteen years ago. Yes, I wanted to scream, I wanted to explain to everyone in the office that I was leaving because the boss had crossed the line, but instead he told the entire company that I 'couldn't handle the stress.' I wanted to make poster-size prints of all the sexual texts I received at three o'clock in the morning and pin them up over his desk. I wanted to die. I wanted him to die. I knew that wouldn't help my career or look good on my résumé. So I confronted him gently. I forgave him. And I'm pretty sure it threw him that I acted with kindness, not punishment. If he's done something since, I'm happy to account for what I experienced, but only on the condition that his other accusers and I are able to help, to see him rehabilitated, so he can walk in a true sense of power, a freedom that he probably hasn't ever experienced. Other than that, I have no desire to slate him in the press or uncover his weakest flaws to people I've never met. That's not justice; that's verbal abuse. I'd be playing him at his own game. And it didn't win me over. Never has, never will."

True justice is found in the wisdom of God, and it's there that we find the courage that often requires suffering. The cross was the ultimate suffering pitted against the core of evil: Satan. In fact, courage *always* requires suffering. This is the whole point of Christianity. To be fully alive. But that can mean some hard choices: suffering nobly, suffering with a good conscience.

More recent incarnations of justice take on the role of God, a holier-than-thou approach to all injustices. This can take many forms: blaming a girl's rape on her short skirt, slandering others' ministries and labeling them heretics, selling hate-provoking baseball caps of presidents, attacking anyone with any opinion on Twitter just to pass the time. Like politicians who refuse to talk to their opposition, it's tiring, dull, and utterly pointless because we're getting nowhere fast. These vengeful tongues, these stories made up by people about leaders they've never met, never conversed with, could be used for so much more.

Where is the lifting up?

Hate abortionists? Then start adopting children.

Hate prejudice? Open your home for educational dinners, where true stories can be heard.

Hate your neighbor? Let's just double-check you're not ever so harsh to yourself too.

Hate what the preachers say? Put down the YouTube channel you've created as a boycott to their ministries and have some private conversations. If they are sincere, they or someone within their ministry will actually talk with you.

Hate the educational secretary for cutting milk? Then start crowdfunding.

Not one injustice is void of an opportunity to lift up, so why aren't we taking it?

It's quicker to shout, to tweet off a quick opinion while we're still in our pajamas. But no atheist will ever feel the urge to convert if they see Christians attack and judge one another. No one wants to spend an evening with the married couple who bicker over dinner. Faith is the greatest guide to processing pain, but few know how to do it. And because they don't do it well, they react, they judge, they seek to hurt the culprit. The noble process pain well and in a way that doesn't harm others.

I've gotten mad when people have treated me poorly. I was part of the parade of girls who, hearing harsh comments made by boyfriends, would start their own smear campaigns, talking to everyone from the worship team to the gardener. I didn't care who heard about it; I just wanted my name to be cleared. If I could have sent locusts to his apartment like God once did, then I would have. That's probably why I wasn't given that supernatural gift. If we can't respond to injustice well, then we can't expect to be given blessings we'd abuse when in pain.

And of course that's where we lose our connection to the truth, to mercy. Ignoring the true pain is where the shame builds. History teaches us that doing the right thing creates a sense of freedom, a sense of conscience that builds our trust. If we act against that wiring to do the right thing, it might, for the moment, feel powerful, but it's never liberating. Instead of confronting our own terror, we try to excuse our vengeful reactions by finding wrathful actions of God in the Old Testament: "Well, if God sent serpents when his people rebelled . . . give me their Instagram account. I'll metaphorically send a legion of frogs through the cunning use of my opinions and a few scriptural references. That'll do the trick."

Did we not read the rest of the Bible? The rest of the New Testament? The epitome of freedom found on the cross? Were the pages stuck together for that part? Something too good on TV?

Where did Christ gauge this new perspective of justice? This merciful side of the Father? In our legalism of the darkest ages, Christ came so we could live in freedom, in the fullness of joy. We missed the memo that fullness of joy requires a fullness of love, which often can form in the choice of vulnerability and pain.

True kingdom justice lifts up the other, if we are humble and brave enough to suffer first. It's the last thing we want to do, but it's the first thing we must do. It's the delivery of flowers to the one who publicly debased us. It's the sharing of communion with the one who destroyed your character in a chapter of their book. It's forgiving the murderer of your son and taking them on as your own. It's blessing the pictures of a bad ex-boyfriend as he marries someone else. It's asking a question before forming assumptions. It's celebrating the colleague when you deserved the promotion. It's the rehabilitation of the sex addict and rescuing the trafficked. It's the standing firm for equality by lifting up the oppressed, the forgotten, the misunderstood.

You may not be facing direct oppression or prejudice, which may mean you're in a privileged position to lift up someone else. We're not in need of the next Martin Luther King Jr. We need everyday Christians to consider carefully their understanding of justice in the context of the New Testament. The one that opposes the control of religion or assumptions. The one that allows inquisitive conversations in the dead of night. The one that allows suffering, a model true Christians remember as they look at the cross. We need a redemption, an awakening to truth that inspired even the centurion who orchestrated Christ's death. The same man who was as used to blood as his paperwork witnessed the utterance of a Christ bleeding and suffocating to death while seeking forgiveness for the Romans gambling over His clothes in front of His mourning and widowed mother. He witnessed the shaking of the very foundations of the earth to Richter scales we can't even calculate, the darkness of the clouds overhead and the temple demolished. In all Christ's perfection the once skeptical and hate-led centurion witnessed the nobility of Christ, and he humbly spoke this revelation: "This man truly was the Son of God" (Mark 15:39 NLT).

When it comes to justice, when there is a truth to be found, God fights for us when we have no breath left to use words.

Justice requires the suffering of our Lord, a case of nobility like no other. It may not be the most appealing invite—to suffer, to surrender. Comradery with the confused crowd is probably more alluring than the loneliness of pioneering a kinder, nobler response. But when you function with an intimacy with the Lord, that ignites the soul in ways nothing else can. Such vulnerable surrender, like being in love, brings life to the lost, the prideful, the hurting. It spends time on the vital matters and refuses to ride on the waves of fear. Let the rest of the world battle over the broccoli and the barren, and ask this taciturn generation to begin to stand for true justice, for the good fight—the one against the accuser who comes to kill, steal, and destroy. For the justice that respectfully perseveres, the one that doesn't hide in fear.

Or cry over spilt milk.

FOR SELF-REFLECTION

The noble consider their responses carefully before executing them. What topics make you the most passionate? Or indeed the angriest?

The noble ask questions before making assumptions. How often do you find yourself making assumptions?

The noble always seek a win-win for injustice. They seek freedom for both sides. When facing adversity, are you able to think about a way to lift the other side up?

The noble don't hide when injustice strikes. Do you hide? If so, how does that manifest? Through keeping busy? Avoiding confrontation? Numbing with unhealthy choices?

The noble suffer sacrifice so the generation to come doesn't have to. Visualize the things you could stand for so those who come after you will have more freedom and emotional health than you do now. What are they?

FROM RIGHTEOUSNESS
TO PERSEVERANCE

A noble posture on righteousness often takes the harder path, therefore perseverance must be our weapon to withstand the toughest storms. If we don't know how to persevere in conflict, in the battle, then we will never discover the amazing outcome of the Lord's strength in us.

"If you're going through hell, keep going."
—WINSTON CHURCHILL

CHAPTER 3

ANNUS HORRIBILIS

PERSEVERANCE

R uby flames began to fill the horizon. I was enjoying an Epsom salt bath when my phone screeched at a pitch I had never heard before. It was an evacuation alert. Half of my city was on fire. I walked outside to ash falling like snow from the sky. People were packing their cars with photo albums, pillows, pet canaries, and children.

This was the beginning of the *annus horribilis*—the horrible year.

Our most valuable possessions sat in our trunks while we waited to return home. During the evacuation, friends began group texting. One by one, people described losing their homes or rushing to the ER with breathing complaints. We clung onto our loved ones as cell signals began to disappear, the power cut off, the sky turned black with emergency vehicles lighting up the darkest smoke. It was as if Armageddon had descended upon

Redding, California. Relatives from across the world attempted to contact us. It must have been bad for our tiny city to have been featured on BBC News.

Family after family bunkered into a friend's house in Carmel, five driving hours south of Redding, refreshing the Internet on our screens every second to see if, indeed, our homes were next. And even then, it wasn't reliable. Red triangles displayed online where the fires were taking place, some directly over our houses, then the red indicators moved and the houses were actually fine. It was like playing Satan's lottery—it felt unpredictably evil. *All that tile work*, I thought. *Burn the house if You must, but not the bathroom, Lord.*

I had just finished renovating my home. My friend's condo, where my goddaughter took her first steps, turned from a palace set for a princess to rubble made of burned roof tiles and a melted cot. Her mother, hearing of the firenado approaching, had prayed around the boundary lines, anointing the circumference of her home with holy oil before running for their lives. Five minutes later, everything, including her wedding dress, became nothing but dust-filled intangible memories. The neighbor's house next door still stood as if nothing had happened. As if the adjacent houses of ash were being overdramatic. The event felt like an inferno of theft. And the news kept coming: a grandmother found dead wrapped around her two grandchildren in attempts to save them from the raging fire that swept in through the back door. People burying themselves in the soil like caterpillars to shelter from the firenado. Most survived. A few didn't.

Many prayers were answered; quite a few were not. At least, not to our mortal measurements.

If you ever wanted to conduct a social or psychological experiment on mankind, this was the week to do it. Some people cried, some rolled their eyes, some made comedy videos about what dining chair to take because they only had room for one (okay, it was me), some were in denial (also me), some sought a type of existentialism—comparing the fires and mudslides in Montecito and Santa Barbara, considering this less impressive. Some switched into Florence Nightingale mode, rallying trucks and aid from nearby cities (not me), some housed other families, and then there were some who ran down the street screaming at quiet houses: "EVERYTHING IS ORANGE!!!" (my assistant, Lila, who also advocates against prejudice based on color; it was an ironic scene to observe).

I stayed in LA for a week, the week that should have been my vacation. Within twelve hours, I came out to the street to find my trunk open and my red suitcase holding my most important valuables stolen—laptop, passport, journals, photos from the sixties of my late father. We were already on heightened alert, and despite the sweet relief of knowing we had at least our lives and our valuables, now we were facing a theft. I could handle the laptop and passport, things that could be replaced, but not the photographs of my father. That felt like a violation. I reached out to my NorCal community, who began praying aggressively as the LA neighborhood began a witch hunt.

For the next eight months, I, along with many friends, would go through the toughest trials since my father died. Pneumonia, an exodus of friends, deaths in the family, the death of my dog (my pseudo child), heartache, disloyalty, depression, adverse reactions and hallucinations caused by antidepressants, fraud, theft again, and delays in my green card (thank you, passport thief). There was no break. Every day brought a new challenge. After eight months of this, I was beginning to really struggle, wondering why God had chosen me to do life at all.

I had heard stories from another dimension of how steadfast the noble were throughout adversity—something that I personally couldn't relate to. How calm and collected they were. How strategic and thoughtfully they still carried out their everyday tasks. Never denying the diffident turmoil they faced but also not pandering to the temptation of victimhood. When Her Royal Highness Queen Elizabeth faced turmoil after the public separation of her son Prince Charles and Princess Diana, the same year that Windsor Castle set alight, I would have dubbed it as the year that "royally sucked." Her correspondents called it the "*annus horribilis.*"

She stated in a speech to the Lord Mayor, "1992 is not a year on which I shall look back with undiluted pleasure."[1] Let's just say I wish I responded with such calculated serenity. My natural responses during that eight months involved growling at every pedestrian, tutting at people in my way. My spare time was spent creating online videos with obvious passive-aggressive sentiments, desperate for the world to stand and agree with me. Any Christian virtues I believed in were not displayed during this time. Those had taken a leave of absence until further notice, and of course this is when people of no faith watch us as Christians, thinking, *Let's see how strong this faith of yours really is.* And although inwardly I could justify my heinous attitude, those on the receiving end just saw a poorly managed emotional spiral. I didn't choose how to respond; I reflexed with venomous quips and a selfish agenda. I responded with pain instead of considered thought.

"You have to set an example of how it is possible to remain effective and dynamic without losing the indefinable qualities, style and character," the queen continued at her luncheon. "We only have to look around this great hall [in Windsor] to see the truth of that." By the end of her televised expression of gratitude to the Lord Mayor and those who offered "fervent" prayers for her, she raised her glass as a toast to the health of the Lord Mayor and Corporation of London.[2]

I wanted to do that. I wanted to be like the queen. This had nothing to do with her real estate. Corgis and castles aside, her stance in the roughest years—the wars, the depression, the destructive affairs the monarchy and country had to face—was always strengthened by her loyalty to the throne. Her diligence in making many difficult decisions, sometimes facing opposition from her own family, was heroic. This was about her relationship with something greater than herself. And if the noble don't have a tangible throne to attest to, they certainly functioned as if they did. Not in some bombastic manner, but in the call of duty.

I wanted to be able to raise a glass to another while I was in pain. I wanted to find ways to praise amid the torture. I wanted to be productive, kind even, when reacting to the *contretemps* of life. For after all, this would exemplify the true test of faith. The concept of being venerable at the toughest times had not been a focus of my attention, until now. If I was about to write a book about this stuff, well, I'd better practice what I penned.

The temptation to burn with fury, to shake my fist at the sky, to question the goodness of God like Job's friends was insatiable. But what good had that done before? It dealt nothing but a bitter aftertaste, robbing me of the hope I once carried. There was something about the conscience's drive to do the right thing. If this was what many people had assumed to be a season of spiritual warfare, well, it was time I took a fresh approach. Instead of running I needed to worship God with my everyday choices.

Boringly predictable, the accuser wanted me to question God's goodness, wanted me to take the easier route, to fall short on the integrity of my choices, seeking solace in the arms of an unsuitable gent. Previous attempts had taught me that playing the cop-out card only leads us to an earlier death, and we'd already had enough of those for 2018. It was game time, and if I was indeed facing the mutts of doom to the doors of my destiny, they'd better buckle up, because I wasn't backing down lightly.

I looked to Paul's advice, finding glory in tribulations. "Knowing that tribulation produces perseverance; and perseverance, character; and character, hope" (Romans 5:3–4). Something I hadn't felt for a while.

To respond with a gospel posture, we intentionally choose our words and actions. Our hearts either jump with glee that we did the right thing, or subtly, and I mean very subtly, the heart takes one step back, unsure if you are reliable to trust in difficult situations. It is hindsight that will tell you if the hearty conscience was on your side. Life will teach you if you are gaining a better relationship with your heart or if you haven't been speaking for years.

Please note, the noble are not robots. They have tough minds but always tender hearts—qualities that Martin Luther King Jr. believed were the difference between the racist and the rational. In the face of adversity, perseverance in pain could look like finding someone to punish, someone to hurt, someone to blame. *Or* it could ask what it can be responsible for, how to face this pain without causing more harm to another, and what role could actually play a part in the solution.

If tribulation is tied to character and character to hope, then I needed to adjudicate what path I wanted to take—the one that got a short-term fix but held no compassion for another's feelings or the gospel, creating nothing but distrust with my own heart; or the one that might suffer in the short term but would cause me to celebrate, looking back, that I had taken the noble choice.

I chose, for a change, option two. But I knew I couldn't do it alone. I can never take the higher road without the wisdom of the Lord, the strength of the Lord, to endure this race entirely with Him.

During a bout of pneumonia I called upon friends, intercessors who rallied around my bed with communion as my sickness ran at a fever pitch. They drank in remembrance the blood of Jesus, while I was coughing up my own. But I needed to surround myself with men and women of greater faith than mine while I was white knuckled and hanging off the cliff edge. I was unable to move at all. And so, during my sickness, like any normal thirty-eight-year-old would do in times of strife, I turned to Tom Cruise.

My housemate returned from work and found me scrambling to change the channel before she caught me with yet another Cruise blockbuster. *Top Gun*, *Cocktail*, *Far and Away*, *Days of Thunder*, *Born on the Fourth of July*. Oh, I lost myself, and by day five of this marathon and housemate glimpsing at the TV screen to murmur, "Oh, Carrie," it was probably a good idea to ask what this overdose of Cruise's filmography was all about. *Perseverance*, I heard the Lord tell me. *The roles he plays show him overcoming and finding victory.* In every tough season, we need to know if we will make it. We look for the survivors; it's why Victor Frankl's *Man's Search for Meaning* was such a hit. And without wishing to sound like a dramatic teenager, I wasn't sure during that time if I would make it. I was never one for working through things. My early days of ballet could account for that.

Any great and noble character in history, any name worth its authority, knew how to persevere. Quitting wasn't an option. It just wasn't. Yet I had been quitting at least on a bi-yearly basis. I ran and ran from diligence in hard work, and from a noble stance in the strife and struggle. If people were unkind at work, I found a new career. If I wasn't getting further ahead, I found a new boss. If I wasn't making an impact on my environment, I got involved in volunteer work until I ran into the same problem. My nomad approach to work and communities left me nothing but a nomad with an undeveloped soul.

The American civil rights movement, Mandela's fight against apartheid, the abolishment of the slave trade, the demise of communism, voting rights for women, the educational system, the urban development of cities, stable families, love-filled marriages, the Dyson vacuum cleaner—none would exist without perseverance.

Such a virtue is found right at the point where you want to run to save your life. The very moment you want to pull away and resist no more is exactly the moment you push through. No one had ever taught me that the self-conquest, the overcoming of the internal battle, is where God's glory is discovered. Where reformation makes its mark. Where reconciliation becomes a possibility again. And I fear we are missing out on this for the next generation. What could be the making of a noble person is being ignored for the sake of comfort, of fear, of ego.

Throughout recent years, millennials have received criticism for dropping out of work. According to many commentators, there is no sustenance in this generation for sticking with things. In response, millennials write articles explaining they just don't see a need to stay in a job that isn't providing satisfaction or sense of purpose. Surely that's wasting their time. I related to argument two. On the cusp of being a millennial, I was inclined to work somewhere for only a year and admit defeat rather than to persevere and stick something out.

"Slasher workers" are on the rise, a description for those who have three job titles: for example, a journalist/web editor/PR person. They are portfolio careerists, and they've been increasing since 2007. You are more likely to recover quickly from redundancy as a slasher with many talents up your sleeve. This is no bad thing. But there is something about the hard graft, the consciousness to not enter into enmity, the willingness to stay in the fight in which you initially wanted to wave a white flag of surrender. It doesn't just affect the career; it's affecting the entire momentum of relationships, purpose, Christianity itself. It creates, if we are not careful, a sense of entitlement. A sense that the world not only owes us, but owes us big time. And when we don't get our way, when we face an *annus horribilis*, we're not raising our glasses in celebration of others, finding whatever is noble or lovely or truthful to hold onto (Philippians 4:8). Instead we're throwing our glasses across the room and asking, *Why us?*

Grit takes a thousand forms, but it is required of us in three major areas: in our calling, in the calamities out of our control (illness, grief, death, rejection), and in our relationships. For a connection with mankind is the most complex and yet most beautiful connection we must persist in. To not fully realize our potential, to not fully armor ourselves when times get tough, to not push into unconditional love when we have been hurt could be the very death of us. If not the death of our character.

Tenacity isn't really just about working through something. We all know too many ambitious characters who bulldoze their way through life, obliterating the feelings and hopes of others. When it comes to the noble, it's more about *how* we work through it—with kindness, patience, thoughtfulness, trust, and self-control (those online passive-aggressive statuses to coworkers or ex-lovers really do need to stop—they don't echo the fruit of the Spirit).[3]

There are a few anchors that can turn the most hideous of hurdles into profound stories:

Vision. Courage. Facing pain. Integrity and, therefore, self-control. But the mighty antidote for all travesty is the something many forget, and that is *prayer*.

The truly noble are those who surrender to unquestionably difficult callings, who face extraordinary brutalities, yet they are walking miracles thanks to prayer.

For example, take Helen Roseveare, a missionary and doctor from Northern Ireland who worked with the Worldwide Evangelization Crusade in the Congo from 1953 to 1973, a time of serious political instability in the early 1960s. She was taken prisoner by rebel forces and remained in captivity for five months, enduring beatings and rapes. After her release she left the Congo but returned two years later to help rebuild the nation. This is the true echo of faith, that despite the gruesome horror of humanity, nothing shall come between our work and our love of the Lord. She was able to disassociate the cruelty of men from the kindness of God. How often we forget to sever the sin with our response in return.

Hostage accounts aside, Roseveare had to contend with many difficulties each day. She once told the story of a night in Central Africa. She was helping a mother in the labor ward, but in spite of their attempts, the mother died, leaving Roseveare with a premature baby and the mother's crying two-year-old daughter. With no electricity to run an incubator and no special feeding facilities, keeping the baby alive would be difficult. Living on the equator didn't mean that nights couldn't be cold; treacherous drafts invaded the ward. A student midwife collected a box they had for these moments and wrapped the baby in cotton wool. Another midwife returned in distress saying their only hot-water bottle had burst while she was filling it. Roseveare instructed the midwives to put the baby as near to the fire as they safely could and to sleep between the baby and the door to keep it from draft's harm.

The following day she prayed with the children of the orphanage. Every day she would give the youngsters suggestions on what to pray over. She told them about the problem of keeping the baby warm with no hot-water bottle. The baby would likely die if it got chilled. She also mentioned the two-year-old daughter in distress because her mother had died. One ten-year-old, Ruth, prayed with a rather blunt consciousness:

"Please God, send us a hot-water bottle. It'll be no good tomorrow God, the baby'll be dead; so please send it this afternoon." Such a prayer made Roseveare gasp. "And while you are about it," Ruth added, "would you please send a baby doll for the little girl so she'll know you really love her?" As faithful as this sounded, Roseveare didn't believe that God could do this. She knew He could do anything, but there were limits, especially in the Congo. Even if someone did send a parcel, who would send a hot-water bottle to the equator?

During the afternoon, a few hours after Ruth's eyebrow-raising prayer, Roseveare received a message that there was a car at the front door. By the time she arrived, the car had gone, but what was left was a large twenty-two-pound parcel. Forty orphanage children gathered around to see. Brightly colored knitted jerseys were passed around to the children. There were knitted bandages for the leprosy patients. The children began to look a little bored. Next a box of raisins and sultanas, perfect for making buns during the weekend. She placed her hand in again and felt something. Could it be? She pulled it out—a brand-new hot-water bottle. She cried after knowing she had not asked God to send it, she had not truly believed that He could. Ruth was front row. "If God has sent the bottle, He must have sent the dolly too!" Rummaging around the box, she pulled out a small, beautifully dressed dolly. "Can I go with you, mummy, and give this dolly to that little girl so she'll know Jesus really loves her?"

The parcel had been on the way for five whole months, packed by Helen's former Sunday school class, whose leader had heard and obeyed God's prompting to send a hot-water bottle, even to the equator. One of the girls had put in a doll for an African child—five months earlier—in answer to the prayer of a ten-year-old that afternoon.[4]

Perseverance requires a childlike faith. And a humbleness that pulls on the one in the room who has more faith than we have. It requires a prayer life that doesn't make logical sense but is an everyday expectation for heaven. Before we call on Him, He is already aware that if you choose to overcome, if you choose to step out, you will need His help. He will answer—before you even present the request. Do everything to avoid bitterness, for it is vexatious to the mind and poisonous to faith. And if life has been cruel, stay with those who have a greater faith than you, even if it comes down to the reliance on a ten-year-old's prayer, for it allows more room for the Lord to display His radical love and takes greater risks for miracles to happen. Our yes to His goodness provides a blank canvas for Him to paint the miracle.

For my own *annus horribilis*, every time I wanted to justify my anger, my bitterness, I made sure someone nearby would keep me accountable. Instead of anger, I chose softness. Instead of hiding, I chose loyal friends. Instead of numbing out on Tom Cruise (I know, I know, it would never have worked), I asked God how He wanted me to respond. I spent time not just sick in bed, but in the secret place. I purposefully avoided men I knew wanted to give me attention, as it wasn't fair to them or to me. I let those who were cruel be cruel. Instead of wanting to arrest the twenty-year-old we watched on security camera take my most valuable possessions, I prayed for him, laying my hands on the screen, crying at the same time. The security team were watching me dumbstruck, perturbed that I would pray for the thief who robbed me of thousands. But Paul was right; it did create character. Because choosing the right heart posture, the right attitude, the kinder attitude built some confidence in the trials, which was a first.

"You've handled this with such patience, with kindness when people have been cruel," my flatmate told me. I was pretty surprised myself. Who knew that asking, *What's the noble response?* would dramatically change my choices? I was far from perfect. But I was now gunning for a character that could choose a response with excellence. That wouldn't excuse itself to the ways of my previous life—the one I waved goodbye to in the funeral of my baptism. I wanted to react with the substance of kindness in all endeavors.

It also dropped my jaw to the floor when I saw how the Lord redeemed all these events.

The stolen red suitcase was found by a local dog walker. Laptop, passport, fountain pens were gone, but the photos of my late father, the things I was really crying over, were still in the suitcase. That felt like a miracle in itself. While reporting the case to LAPD, I was reminded of how Joseph responded in his captivity, in Genesis 37–50. Not once did he question—in the misunderstandings, in the wrong convictions, in the betrayal of his own brothers—why the Lord hadn't protected him, why the Lord hadn't delivered him from jail. Joseph was so focused on what God was doing that he didn't have time to focus on what He wasn't doing. A happy similarity to Daniel. And again with Paul, the same man who during imprisonment advised the early church to "glory in tribulations" (Romans 5:3). The same man who had faced shipwrecks, betrayal, physical ailments, hunger, betrayal again, disappointments of other church leaders, bereavement, apostasy, unemployment, snake bites, rejection, beatings, at least two years of captivity, and rioting had enough authority to speak for the case of perseverance. And tell us how to persevere. Not with complaints, but with nobility. To encourage the captain with hope in the face of a shipwreck, to be long-suffering in the face of betrayal. To allow people to make their own choices, to ask for help in ill health, to trust that food is coming, to *gently* confront poor behavior, to find God's comfort when death has robbed us of a loved one, to trust that God will help us financially. He told us in how he shirked off the snake that bit into the hand and continued to speak to the crowd, how he praised God during the beatings, and witnessed to those who robbed him of his freedom.

We're given enough stories of how to behave during intense hardship.

So why don't we do it?

Control and, therefore, fear. An inability to process pain effectively. Poor modeling didn't give us a great head start (which is what is so beautiful about Scripture; you're given another option). Lack of patience. The need for approval of mankind over the approval of our Lord. A lack of identity, coming from a spirit of orphanship, unaware that the spirit of adoption is fully alive in you. Unaware of who your dad is. Not enough Tom Cruise films accessible on your TV (I jest, of course).

When the noble persevere, they set the stage for the grand finale. The testimonies of God's brilliance. For the red suitcase found by a dog walker. For the reconciliation of friends who apologized for their hurts. For the millions raised for the people affected by the Carr Fire, for the $48,000 given to me alone for fire damage to my house. For the swift healing of pneumonia that allowed me to fly on a mission trip to New York. When we showed up, we found Him healing people—legs that grew in front of our eyes. Memory loss recovered. Backs aligned. Staff workers for a homeless shelter able to move their right rotators again. Family reconciliation.

For the twenty-five awful things I had faced in one year, I had hundreds of testimonies of God's goodness.

When the two hundred thousand acres of fire tried to engulf Redding, much of the city was protected by diligent firefighters. They had become our heroes. Signs hung across bridges, buildings, and homes shouted praise for their courageous feats. Hundreds began to ash-out the homes of those who had lost everything. Boiler suits and HEPA masks became our usual attire. It felt strange to rummage through another person's property, but when life hits you with such shocking blows, your vulnerability adjusts to a hope for help, greater than any pride.

One couple stood at the foundation lines of their home, with a paper plan of how it used to be.

"Is there anything you lost that you would like us to find?" one volunteer asked.

"Yes. My late mother gave me her diamond wedding ring, and it was my most precious possession. But we didn't have time to take anything. You're just running for your life by that point." The wife teared up. A silence hit the volunteers, unsure what to say, or how to even comfort, as they looked over the ash and broken terra-cotta tiles. A hopeless task. But the team prayed. Then we began the hours of shifting and shoveling, handful by handful, as we searched for anything that looked remotely like an identifiable object. These ash-outs were taking place all over the city. Focusing on someone else during a difficult time seemed to be an effective antidote to the grief. Shelby, a student of mine, was on the team that day. She was thorough, excellent in her work and approach, and detailed in observation, even though sweat was pouring down her face in the one-hundred-degree heat. One person shoveled ash onto a fine grate that two other people sifted through, picking out coins, war medals, anything that hadn't melted into unrecognizable plastic.

"Wait!" Shelby shouted. "Is that—?!"

She picked it up, a piece of metal, circular, with a dim but distinctive stone.

"Hey! *Hey!*" she called for the team leader.

The team leader ran over. Not wishing to get the owner's

hopes up, he calmly walked over to the homeowner to show her the object.

Shelby saw the woman fall to her knees, crying with overwhelming thankfulness. It was the diamond ring she thought was lost forever.

This is our God.

The One who brings you people in the most torrid times of pain. The God who finds diamonds in the ashes. The One who teaches you to be kind in a world full of cruelty. The One who holds back the unduplicated photographs from the thief. The One who strengthens you if you'll only say yes. The One who is mightier than the fires, the deaths, the disappointments.

The ignoble may persevere, but the noble prepare their journeys with humility, wisdom, courage, sacrifice, and trust in a God who provides a hot-water bottle five months before you need it.

On leaving one of the ash-outs, we saw a sign in the driveway of a house still standing on the opposite side of the street. Handwritten were the words: WE RAN FOR OUR LIVES, YOU RAN IN WITH YOURS. THANK YOU, FIRST RESPONDERS.

It's time for Christianity to show what the grit of the gospel is truly made of: diamonds, healing, hot-water bottles, and heroism.

Our only job is to show up.

FOR SELF-REFLECTION

Christianity wasn't created to hide us and keep everyone safe; it was created so we could be fully alive. Hiding from a tough season won't build character.

The noble take on the tough times as opportunities, chances to celebrate God's strength.

The noble pray—a lot.

The noble make enough room in their lives. They offer up a metaphorical blank canvas in prayer that asks for Him to show up in miraculous ways. Despite previous disappointments, they still seek His face and ask what He is doing in their circumstances.

The noble find the one with the most faith in the room if they are currently struggling themselves.

The noble keep their integrity even in difficult seasons and never use a tough time to excuse poor behavior.

In their ability to face adversity with grace, gentleness, kindness, and honesty, the noble add more trust and a sense of confidence with themselves and the Lord.

They don't let pride twist them into isolation. They reach out to their communities.

They actually process pain, facing it head on, allowing the Lord to comfort and guide them.

They find ways to celebrate, to pour into others, to be a source of hope to those around them, even in the roughest years.

How do you respond to tough times? How would you like to respond better?

Do you have a committee of people who hold more faith than you? If not, who might be on your committee?

Do you have accountability to ensure you thoughtfully respond, rather than react to the hurdles? If not, how can you find it?

Instead of questioning God's goodness, are you asking what He is doing in the situation? Take a scenario you are struggling with, ask what He is doing and, then, what you can do to proceed with noble strength.

FROM PERSEVERANCE
TO INTEGRITY

There's perseverance, and then there is sheer willpower. It's not the goal that you accomplish so much as to how you get there; one way could bless those around you, another way could obliterate them. Even for Job, when everything was lost, it was his integrity that held him strong in the darkest hour. Whichever path we choose reflects the true composition of our souls.

"Do you still hold fast to your integrity?"
—JOB 2:9

CHAPTER 4

EMPERORS OF TRUTH

INTEGRITY

You could cut the air with a chainsaw. It was May 2005, and Andy Roddick was facing match point to win against Fernando Verdasco. If he got this, not only would he win the match, but he'd be breaking the seven-game winning streak that Verdasco was currently basking in. The second serve was struck. The umpire announced Roddick the winner as Verdasco hit a second fault. The court cheered, but Roddick showed no display of celebration, walking instead to the spot where the ball had apparently hit outside of the line. There was silence. Roddick called the linesman and showed him that the play was actually inside the line.

How many times have we seen sportsmen fight against an umpire? Roddick included. But it's usually for their own sakes, not the opponents'. But on this occasion the crowd and the commentators couldn't believe it. What was he doing?

He could have stood on the mark. He could have kept silent. But he decided to save the umpire a trip down to the court. He acted according to his integrity. We've all avoided the truth for the sake of an enjoyable life. Again, just a millisecond decision can change the entire cosmos of our destiny, or as for Roddick, his bank balance, his sponsorships, his fame, his gilded trophies. His formidable sportsmanship, his honest move actually cost him tens of thousands of dollars as Verdasco went on to win the match.

Truly noble gents encompass an air of integrity, one that carries a brutal honesty, one that at times costs dearly. Integrity is something I long for in a husband. Something I don't find as often as I would like. Everyone seems to be pretty aware when it comes to the liable behavior. Actions like those from the wolves on Wall Street become a cautionary tale for anyone else considering an occupation in fraud. In regard to integrity, I'm not referring to the big guns—the fraudsters, the adulterers, the Robin Hoods of the world (he was still a thief, no?). Nor would I reference the Howard Sterns of America—those willing to say or do anything to entertain their audience. Stern recently apologized to the *Hollywood Reporter* for being such a "jerk." No, I'm referring to the subtle, the discreet gestures that don't have to be acted upon, but with the noble, it's an intrinsic trait to choose the truth over the internal desires and self-pleasurable wins.

In fact, in this current cultural climate, we are actually down on "toxic behaviors." The statistics showing some interesting results.

Gen Z are known as go-getters, activists, the big dreamers. It's beautiful, it's bold, and I'm intrigued to see what nifty little surprises are up their sleeves when they rule the earth. They are drinking less, smoking less, shooting up less, and avoiding teenage pregnancy. But I'm searching for the small actions, the everyday exchanges that care for the well-being of the other, without seeking our own needs being met.

According to some reporters, one reason why these numbers

are plummeting quicker than Madonna's reputation on the *Blonde Ambition* tour is the smartphone. Their time is swallowed up with videos of other people's antics: a kid kicking his dad, some dude popping a wheelie on a speedway bike in front of a cop car, a girl using a shotgun for the first time and it backfiring to the point of nearly shooting herself. The response? Hysterical laughter. I like a joke, but not when it's the dismantlement of a child's face. I'm delighted there is less focus on Bacardi rum and Marlboro investments than there was in the nineties. Take it from me in my twenties—they really do scupper the scent of your bedroom in the morning, never mind your lungs. But I'm just not sure those lowered statistics are the result of a belief system that prioritizes integrity.

The change in behavior isn't because of a moral shift but because of distractions. No one made a conscious effort to have more integrity. The increase in STDs is probably a sign of that.

The most perturbing part of all? In my experience, people who have integrity are not always Christians. Instead, I've found many an unbeliever's loyalty to honesty stronger than the conviction of some believers. If we don't truly wish to live a real and personal relationship with God, we'll do what I did—adjust the Scripture to fit with our lifestyle and our societal expectations. We'll seek the easier life. We'll join with Christians who have less desire to walk in truth. We come to church to get fed by community, by an inspiring sermon, by worship for an hour a week, then sleep with our boyfriends at night. Of course this doesn't apply to everyone, but this discord between faith and walking it out is increasing.

The real tests of our doctrine are always found in the difficult encounters with life itself. I've lost count of how many times, for example, students have told me how much they love the Lord, how they spend *hours* with Him, but were completely unaccountable to anyone, including myself (their pastor). They'd swipe in for attendance at school but rock off to the lake for the day. They'd talk about the importance of serving but would be too busy talking to their friends to help someone struggling to stack the chairs next to them.

Integrity does not come in the grand challenges; it's a 24/7 job that, for the noble, becomes second nature. It prioritizes the truth.

When it comes to Jesus lovers and their romance, statistics have said that atheists lie less than Christians when it comes to the world of online dating.[1] To get our needs met, we're lying about our height and our jobs. If we're going to lie about the very basics, we've already lost trust. We didn't just represent the Lord poorly; we didn't even represent ourselves well. Should we be cutting our conscience just to fit in with this year's fashions? I thought our Christianity was serving the Author of Time, not serving our own needs. The autonomy of the Internet is not helping us.

Noble integrity is composed of a few things, the first being honesty. Not just when it's required, but anytime we have an opportunity to be honest, as Roddick did. It's a hunt for truth, while saving ourselves and others from deceit.

It makes me think of a friend of mine, probably the best example of a man with integrity I know. This next story may not match the grand description I just labeled him with, but you'll note that building integrity starts with the smallest of incidents. He echoes the heart behind Luke 16:10: "He who is faithful in what is least is faithful also in much; and he who is unjust in what is least is unjust also in much."

"I think you've undercharged me for this packet of chewing gum." My friend smiled.

The cashier checked the receipt. *Undercharged?* My friend was right. She had charged him ten cents less than the retail price. She had also seen the Aston Martin Virage he just stepped out of. *Cars like this don't typically belong to a guy arguing over being undercharged for a chewing gum packet*, she thought. *Either that car isn't his, or there*

are those out there who think that sweating the small stuff is honorable.
For the record, the car didn't establish his identity. If it had, I doubt
he'd have even checked the transaction. But the others in the shop
were trying to weigh what was going on here. The cashier asked
for the manager to come over, unsure what to do.

"You can just keep the dime," the manager replied.

"Thank you very much, but I'd rather pay it. If I make sure
you get what belongs to you, He'll [pointing upward] make sure
I get what belongs to me."

He smiled and hopped back into his car.

Neither the manager nor the cashier could believe that one
so wealthy would insist on paying an amount easily lost down
the back of the sofa. Something within this exchange echoed
the integrity of the noble. The intrinsic behavior that tells me,
"I'll know what you believe in by what you do." He believed in
truth, and the right for everyone to live in truth. To undermine a
company by even one cent wasn't acceptable or honorable.

Please note, he was willing to be laughed at, willing to
confront (kindly) the status quo, the normal expectancy, while
bringing honesty to a whole new standard. How many in that
shop, even just for a minute, stopped to think about their own
integrity? How many were questioning if they were being that
thorough or just flying through life without much thought?
There is always time for integrity.

Albert Einstein said, "Whoever is careless with the truth in
small matters cannot be trusted in important affairs."[2] The same
man who stayed true to the price of a packet of chewing gum
also leads one of the most pivotal revival movements in Western
Christianity. There's something about how we steward the small
moments that builds a trust with our Lord so that we may handle
the responsibility that comes with an abundance of blessings.

And I don't wish to frighten you here, but if you remember,

when it came to Ananias and Sapphira in the book of Acts, telling an inaccurate fib about how much they had given to the early church, it didn't work out too well for them (Acts 5). I'm not suggesting in our case that we'll drop dead, but insincerity like this is a killer of trust, a killer of unity, a killer of clear thinking with the Lord.

Admit it. If you saw someone display such honesty, such diligence, such precision, you'd want to hire him or her. Heck. You'd trust that person with your life if you witnessed it often.

Integrity trumps the desperate need to please with the desperate need to be truthful. It's uncomfortable, confrontive, painful, real, and undyingly intoxicating to witness. It doesn't cut in front of the line, it doesn't criticize, it doesn't seek attention, it doesn't require money to puff up the identity, as in the story of Ananias and Sapphira; it doesn't need to win, it refuses to say yes just because everyone else does, it doesn't control, it confesses sin even if it will hurt. Truth must always override the intimidation of pain.

Some of Christ's strongest rebukes were to people who were lying to themselves: Peter when he was in denial regarding Jesus' destiny, the Pharisees' religious denial and the hypocrisy of their actions versus their beliefs. Yet how encouraged Christ became when the Samaritan woman at Jacob's well spoke truthfully about her current living situation with a man. It was her ability to speak truth that allowed Christ to bring her complete breakthrough.

Whether it's as significant as an unhealthy lifestyle or as small as an undercharged packet of Wrigley's, we are given invites to see if we will show up in the name of truth and nothing but the truth, to see if we truly understand the character of our God.

I speak as if from the pulpit, but little did I know how much my chicanery some years ago would slowly lead me down dangerous paths. How else do you think I learned this?

When I began working in the film industry, I received a fair bit of favor, especially from the men. I was twenty-one and naive.

I didn't believe in myself and had no clue what I stood for; I was unaware that those two things go hand in hand. I took advantage of whatever was given to me. Some called it orphan thinking; some called it greed. At the time I called it insecurity.

A particular film director spotted me on set during production. He began to invite me to dinners, to parties with the stars. As the friendship grew, I opened my door to his assistant handing me the director's entire film collection on DVD with a brand-new DVD player to watch them on. I was offered a paid-for session with a reputable photographer to take my headshots, and I happily accepted the offer. When the photographer asked me to pull the strap down from the shoulder of my vest top, I looked to my friend, and realized I was crossing the line of my modesty into some sordid play for attention. I obliged and walked home in shame. Nothing was exposed, just a bare shoulder, but crop the photo and it was enough to know I was acting against my own standards.

I didn't have the guts to say no or the honesty to confront the director. In fact, I kept being his friend. I didn't have enough integrity to say no. I had access to the elite. To the ones whose face graffitied the walls of thousands of girls! This wasn't hurting anyone. Besides, it might be my last chance to be surrounded by the glitterati. It's here you can tell I'm borderline millennial, where we score 25 percent higher on entitlement-related issues than forty- to sixty-year-olds. It's why I would often leave any integrity I did have locked up and tucked away at home.

The noble trust in something more than fate or opportunity. Something greater than celebrity, a rich man, a goal of success. They trust in God. His abundance. His attention. His love. His wisdom. His knowledge. His unfailing strength.

No love affair occurred with this director. I managed to avoid being on my own with him, but I did keep saying yes to the invites, and finally, when he asked me what I would do if a film director should ever propose the role of a lifetime to me on the condition I slept with him one night, I knew I had a chance to say something.

"Judi Dench never had to sleep with someone to do well in the industry. And if she didn't have to, neither should I."

You might think I deserved a standing ovation—well done me for speaking the truth, for avoiding temptations. But already I'd given fodder for him to lose respect. He already had pictures of the bare shoulder, he already had dined me and enjoyed my company for months. I wasn't acting with integrity, and my actions weren't reflecting my words.

I didn't hear anything more from the director. Perhaps rightly so. I'd given mixed messages and never been truly honest with him. I was taking advantage of his status as much as I was being taken advantage of in my naivety.

I decided from that point on, unless I was romantically interested in someone, I wouldn't take their presents. No DVD players, jewelry, or gifts, unless they were going to be a long-term friend and we both knew exactly what the status of the relationship was.

Of course, I might have *decided* to act upon these new convictions, but integrity is tested in the tougher stretches and has to be truly *acted out* before we can know for sure we possess it. And it was tested a few years ago when I was suffering from serious sinus infections. Sounds rather pathetic, but we couldn't work out what was bringing on the fever and lethargy. I had spent thousands, and I mean thousands, visiting different doctors. I traveled to LA, hoping I'd find answers with a friend's doctor in Beverly Hills. By now the payments were going onto credit cards, and debt was piling up. Choosing a career path as a pastor in my midthirties meant my salary had decreased to what I was earning at twenty-three. I wasn't going to be able to pay this debt back anytime soon.

Waiting in the doctor's office, I began talking to a music producer who asked if I wanted to take a look around his recording studios. He seemed kind and genuine, so I took him up on the offer the next day. The studios were some of the finest in Hollywood; clearly he was packing a few bob, and I could feel that money had played a major part to his position in society. Over dinner he asked about my doctor's visit, and I told him how much I missed the National Health Service in England, how much cheaper the whole journey would have been.

"I'd like to pay off your medical bills," he nonchalantly delivered over a Philadelphia roll.

I was relieved, delighted. *This must be the favor of the Lord!* I thought to myself. *I knew God would turn this tragedy into greatness. A joy for mourning . . .* and all those scriptural references you can think of where the Lord wishes to relieve you from American Express debt.

Except it wasn't the Lord.

I had worked too hard on my discernment to know that this generous guy had had women clawing at his wallet since he was a young kid. The Enemy's lies had told him all he was ever good for was his money, and I didn't want to reinforce that.

"Wow, that's so kind. I'm taken aback that you would want to offer me so much when you've known me for only a couple of days."

"Yeah, well, I'm a good guy, and I have the money, so just take it."

"Problem is—" I choked on a fish egg. "I can't take it. I actually don't think it's right to take money from you, even if you wouldn't notice. It's so kind, but I don't think I'm supposed to."

He put his chopsticks down. "No girl has ever declined money from me."

"Yes, I wondered about that. I'd rather be the woman who lets you feel respected as a friend than as some ATM machine."

You might think I felt great about the whole exchange, defiantly standing on my firm morals, standards that could weather the storm. But I was panicked. Had I blown my chance? Was that conviction I felt? Or fear?

A week later, I returned to my students, who gave me a gift bag. Inside was $1,000 in cash with a note saying, "We hope it helps." Their collection made me explode into tears. It wasn't the full amount, but that didn't matter. It was the underlying message God was trying to tell me that hit me right in the gut.

Christ and His companions had such a trust in provision, such a profound belief that all would be taken care of, because they were working always for a greater good, for truth, something outside of time and their own space. Standing for what is right meant they could deny, turn down, disengage with the charming trappings of a material world. When they are lacking, struggling, these are precisely the moments when the noble take stock of what they truly believe in. It has to be rooted, established in you in a way that ensures you're a lighthouse in the storm. You're a solution to a problem, not a victim of it.

Think again of Joseph. Already betrayed and misunderstood by his brothers, already enslaved to Potiphar, and unmarried. Genesis explains how the Lord was with Joseph, a hard thing to believe after all that had happened to him. But there was favor on him in Potiphar's household. Potiphar trusted every project he handed to Joseph because it always prospered in his hand (Genesis 39). It didn't help that ol' Joe was handsome in form and appearance.

Joseph, no doubt, faced temptations. Perhaps to revolt, to escape, and to be intimate with a woman. Potiphar's wife on more than one occasion attempted to seduce him when he was alone. Joseph declined. Unlike me, he didn't take the invites to cavort. He knew he was exposed to danger when he was in the house alone without anyone around. Potiphar's wife caught him by his garment, telling him to sleep with her. He was aware of the trust bestowed on him by Potiphar and so legged it—leaving his cloak behind. She screamed out to the household that Joseph was trying to assault her, mocking her behind her husband's back. She used the cloak as proof, and Potiphar responded with anger.

This was a crime that usually ended in execution.

So why did Potiphar put Joseph in jail? Why didn't he execute him? Might I humbly suggest that it was Joseph's noble character, his track record with integrity that saved his life? He was a man who held to the truth in all the small tasks, a man who ministered and poured into others, a man who cared for his master, a man who held the divine favor of the Lord and, therefore, never played victim. When you're known for your integrity, it's difficult to believe such accusations.

Is this the gift of running from temptation? Building trust like this can sometimes, even literally, save our own lives.

Joseph, in his perseverance, learned of the importance of self-awareness, to not boast of his own dreams in front of a crowd who couldn't handle it (notably, his brothers). Over time he learned to focus on others, and with such self-awareness, knew of his shortcomings.

Another component of integrity is honor. Not charm, not a performance of martyrdom, but kindness with genuine motivation. A person with integrity confronts instead of bickering behind people's backs. He or she asks questions instead of making assumptions. Which, in turn, avoids offense and unnecessary confusion. People with integrity are truthful to themselves, never hiding behind charm or self-deceit. It's phenomenal how much we can believe our own hype. And in the digital era, where the morose gains more attention than good deeds, where performance is rarely caught out from its authentic agenda, there's incentive to just lavish in the limelight—but we aren't always fooled. And the wisest spot a "kind gesture" as compared to a genuine one.

Each Tuesday Mother Teresa would take donations at the

altar for the Home for the Destitute and Dying. People would line up with small sums of money, coins, notes, and maybe even checks. On one particular Tuesday, she noticed a company of men had suited up for this occasion. Accompanying them was a film crew. They were carrying one of those large checks—you know the ones, the ones you would not fit into an SUV even if you put the back seats down. They were donating a substantial amount of money to Mother Teresa's Home for the Destitute and Dying. She shook hands with everyone in the line, taking her time with each donor, thanking them for the generosity and sacrifice. They thought she might pay more attention to them, considering this was going to be the mother of all donations (no pun intended). But she asked them to stay in line, like everyone else.

They surrendered to her orders, checking each other's excitement, straightening their ties. Camera's ready? *Here we go . . . it's soon our moment.*

But when it was their turn, she took the check, placed it on the altar, and shouted, "Next!"

They were a little perturbed. Another person watching her from the sidelines found the courage to enquire, "Mother, I'm sorry to interrupt but these men traveled a long way to give you money, and you weren't quite as grateful as you had been toward the other lesser sums of money. Is something wrong?"

"For as long as those cameras are on, you're not doing this for the right reason. So there won't be a thank you from me."

Busted.

If this company had wanted to build a friendship with the Mother, they had another thing coming. For there can be no friendship without honor, no friendship without confidence, and no confidence without integrity.

It's not just about doing the right thing, or doing the honest thing, but a game of checking the heart—every time. And as much as we would love to think that the world cannot gauge the inner workings of our minds, the prophetic can, and the most brilliant will. They sense an insecurity created by entitlement miles off; they cling tight to the steadfast over the charmers, the generous over the greed, the sincere over the irreverent.

It's important to know that telling yourself the truth is actually integrity. Honesty is telling the truth to other people. And you can't do one without the other.

Principles of integrity are all well and good. But why isn't there more integrity in the world? Why isn't everyone noble in this area? It is dependent on a few things. The first is what you believe your identity to be. Who modeled this for you, if anyone did at all? Are you functioning in life with a fear of abandonment or lack of provision? If so, you're likely to still want to have your needs met; then the kingdom will probably look for someone else to carry out their work. Any trigger from a previous wound can easily make kindness toward another less likely.

Another factor of nobility is intimacy. As a little girl, I would always see if my dad was watching when I was about to do something impressive on the playground (a cartwheel in this instance). It wasn't worth it if Daddy wasn't watching. And in these sweet exchanges of kindness, or doing the right thing over the wrong, I take a little wink at Pops even today, hoping, wishing, praying that I made Him smile. Better yet, that I caught Him off guard.

Job's intimacy with His Lord was exactly what nursed Job through the most treacherous period of his life. Even his wife questioned why he would stay honest and honorable when he had lost everything, including his children and his health. But this was the sign of his great character; it didn't keep him from having questions. It never voids anyone of pain. But what a trust of obedience, what a remarkable account of solidarity in Job's love for God, to never sway, to not falter in his faith just because things hadn't gone well. Job waited upon the Lord, never changing behavior, working this out behind closed doors. It is just a matter of time until we see the fullness of the decisions we made, but don't expect to always see them this side of eternity. In the dismissal of the crowd's applause, there is always a cloud of witnesses waiting to celebrate those who stood true to their faith when no one else was watching.

Here's what integrity doesn't do: It doesn't pretend. It doesn't waste time looking in the mirror. It doesn't misuse a handicap badge for a closer parking spot when the driver is fully abled. It doesn't lie about its height. It doesn't ignore the requirements of others in the room. It doesn't follow the herd. It doesn't buckle under pressure.

So the Lord is looking for the ones who will stand up when it's most inconvenient. To sit in the lion's den or to dance in the fire (as Daniel and Shadrach, Meshach, and Abed-Nego did). He's hoping we'll call the ball "in" when the world hoped it was out (as Roddick did). He wants you to quit the overtly charming yet empty marital promises with a girl you only met last week. He's looking for the teachable, the accountable, the ones who still speak highly of their heartbreakers. It might be as minute as following through on a promise you made to take your kid go-karting, or it could be as courageous as refusing to deny Christ when a gun is to your head. Whatever it may look like, whatever treacherous scenario our wildest adventures invited us into, when we glue our actions to our words, when we harmonize our behavior with our values, it's astonishing what can occur, what destiny unfolds before us. Oh, the mountains you can move, because you learned to hear God first on how to carry away the small stones.

It's time we stop deceiving ourselves, myself included, with puffed-up stories, with self-delusional filters, with denial, with downplaying the importance of the subtle gestures that grow our character. When we do these things, we lose the opportunity to be the salt, to be the light.

As believers in the King who invented this stuff, isn't it worth giving His approach a shot?

What will it be? A case for the ego? For pride? Or could it be that through choices made with integrity, through kind moments that set us apart from the common expectations of the world, we finally build a case for Christ, for the teachings that so uniquely set Him apart?

One tiny packet of gum at a time.

FOR SELF-REFLECTION

Integrity begins small.

If we are intentional with integrity, we will build trust with ourselves and with our Lord.

If this has not been modeled for us in our upbringing, then community and friends are important to keep us accountable.

Consider the result of the choice you're about the make. What will be the outcome of the choice you make?

Is fear of letting go of control a reason for you to hold on to the easier option rather than make the harder choice?

Have you checked your receipt? Are you just in your actions when it doesn't benefit you?

Are you choosing truth over popularity, over discomfort, over your own needs being met?

FROM INTEGRITY TO HUMILITY

Although we can speak the truth and find
ways to move mountains, carrying one
stone at a time, humility must always be
threaded throughout integrity. We can't
learn God's ways of integrity if we are not
humble enough to hear His teachings.

CHAPTER 5

"FROM NOW ON, ONLY THE PILOT CAN FLY THE PLANE"

HUMILITY

I am more powerful than the solar system."

The note was on my colleague's desk, an affirmation he had written for himself. You'd think I'd blush at the audacity, but actually, this was the world of advertising, aka my workplace. Usually malapert, usually abrasive, usually resilient to your wife running off with a wealthier man. Affairs were as common as desk staplers. Cruel pranks and cocaine were part of the morning meetings. We were the mavericks who persuaded an entire nation to vote conservative after a very successful advertising campaign in the '80s. Such success might have drawn some of the country's greatest creatives, but it also provided a hotbed for growing egos.

Bloodshed from physical fights might have been evident in the boardrooms, but we were the invincible think tank of the creative world, the playground where actors, directors, writers, and *Vogue* all skipped together. I relished in its exuberance, dined out on the crazy stories, and believed in this faux glory . . . for about seven minutes.

We were paid to draw attention to ourselves (sure, sometimes the client's product too), to be impressive, gaining vast amounts of money for it. So it made sense that when a reputable production company flew a small plane into the Amazon jungle to film the territory of an aboriginal tribe who had never set sight on a dentist, you would expect to hear in inebriated tones, "Okay! From now on, only the pilot gets to fly the plane!"

We believed we were so invincible that we could fly. Without a license. Or sobriety in that case.

If we got something wrong, we'd point fingers, make up terrible excuses, or, worse yet, create some barbaric diversion to distract from the fact that we were humans who made mistakes. I seem to remember someone dressing up as Sherlock Holmes on one of these occasions. People developed reputations for all sorts of outrageous actions, while I developed a reputation for crying in the restroom five times a day.

True story.

I mention these decadent days because within this charming but ignoble case of lunatics taking over the asylum, I longed for nobility. The disciplined, the courteous, the tender, the humble, the sacrificial—words so far from the world I worked in. It was during this time that the kindness of Christ, the One I had left a long time before, began to draw me back. The glossy world of comradery wasn't so glossy anymore. Like with my friends who had worked in the Peace Corps, who witnessed the effects that the occult had in their line of work and began to seek the light for respite. For me, the arguments for or against Jesus' incarnation were neither here nor there. Dawkins's *God Delusion* didn't provide me the relief I needed, the relief that was Jesus' rationale for kindness and unconditional love.

It was the ego that was shifting our behavior in the workplace, hindering us all from being civil, much less noble, and it was my industry that encouraged it.

Before I worked for my boss, he once threw a yucca plant through the office window because he was told he couldn't hire a particular film director for a new commercial. Tantrums—just your regular rock 'n' roll lifestyle. No biggie. He was fired the next day. Also no biggie. But when the story got around the industry quicker than the Anglo-Zanzibar War (it lasted thirty-eight minutes), another CEO from another agency hired him immediately. You see, he loved his passion. The bigger the ego, the bigger the reward. Integrity, humility, thinking of the *consequences* of throwing a yucca plant through a window, were never rewarded; they were walked over.

Yes, the Pencil awards, the Lion awards, the VIP passes to Cannes Festival, the "Ooh, what's this?" goody bags, the dinners at Cecconi's, the Bentleys, the Moët, the part-time lovers, the drugs (I would excuse myself by highlighting my allergy to aspirin) were all part of the agency's job description, but I wondered how I ended up working in a place that cared more for products than people. I was oddly mesmerized by the arrogance, the sheer unapologetic self-belief that bordered on not just ruthlessness but transgressed to narcissism at its finest. The only thing we got hot under the collar for was our reputation. Feeding the ego was as addictive as the spending sprees and late-night parties. None of this led to life though. For many, it led to the opposite—quite literally.

Amid this heinous atheistic chaos was a tiny conscience—my tiny conscience—aware that this lifestyle, the one that everyone wanted, wasn't hitting the true depths of the soul. The part of us that longs for meaning, for something beyond ourselves, beyond the solar system.

Even though I was yet to come back to Christ, I remember wanting to keep hold of this feeling, this sense of being tiny, so that I didn't become numb to life, the world, and the people in it. I designed a floor tile to place just below my desk. I asked our graphic designers to create something that looked like an engraving on the floor and had it printed.

It read:

> He has filled them with skill to do all manner of work of the engraver and the designer and the tapestry maker, in blue, purple, and scarlet thread, and fine linen, and of the weaver—those who do every work and those who design artistic works. (Exodus 35:35)

"How narcissistic," one project manager noted as he embedded a muddy shoe print into the tile. I smiled and thought, *You missed the whole point.* We were unteachable, stubborn, and stuck to our own concrete, immovable opinion, and it's why we couldn't grow or hang onto relationships. If only I had also printed on the floor tile: "The wise in heart will receive commands, but a prating fool will fall" (Proverbs 10:8).

I had believed that satisfying the ego, that attempting to be someone else instead of myself was the ticket to long-lasting satisfaction and far easier than being myself. If I was making an impact, I was useful, powerful, and productive, which, therefore, was my permission to exist. *To live, you must earn it* . . . said Christ never.

Today we are introduced to new generations labeled as narcissists. And to be clear, even though I'm an advocate for taking ownership, in this case, I don't think it's their fault. It's what we've fed them. My former workplace unquestionably contributed to that—without intention. Three times as many middle school girls want to grow up to be a personal assistant to a famous person as want to be a Senator, according to a 2007 survey; four times as many would pick the assistant job over CEO of a major corporation, just to be closer to being "in."[1] Professor Paul Harvey, of the University of New Hampshire, carried out a series of studies measuring psychological entitlement and narcissism on a group of Gen-Yers and found they scored 25 percent higher than respondents ages forty to sixty and 50 percent higher than those over sixty-one.[2]

It seems humility is becoming a lost art form. It's certainly not a virtue people love seeking out.

Some scholars believe that the rise in narcissism has its roots in cultural changes, especially increased focus on individualism. It comes from sources like advertising, from parents' experience of their own parents with restricted allowances to dream of being an actor versus a lawyer, from society as a whole placing a greater value on young people's individual achievement over their civic duty.

Then there are the stories I've personally observed of the younger generation. Their desire to confront some authority in their life to let their "heart have a voice," when really that conversation was only beneficial for the kid instigating the confrontation, while the adult leaves deflated, hurt, and confused. They refuse to help at their local church—be it stacking chairs or setting up the sound equipment, because "it's not part of their ministry." Naturally, confronted with such entitlement, I've wanted to grab a Bible and place their noses in Acts 28. You know what I'm going to say—the part where Paul is adding kindling to a fire, just after a shipwreck I might add, and it touches on the helping bit—you know, the bit that's not "part of your ministry." In that chapter, Paul is bitten by a mad viper that launched from the heat of the fire onto his hand, and not only did he not make a ditty and dance about it (something I can't confirm I wouldn't do), but the crowd marveled that he was healed from the bite, just before he began to speak. *Do you think, my friend, that such a small helping action as adding wood onto the fire was part of his ministry?* I think so.

We're a far cry from nobility if we are refusing to humble ourselves enough to stack the chairs.

I've witnessed students become bitter after a pastor challenged them on an inappropriate behavior that was hurting other people. I have to remind them that I bleed too. Instead of being teachable, we human beings tend to revolt against wisdom that could actually help us grow, because our egos have made it unbearable to be wrong. We're scared the correction means we are unlovable. That we aren't special. Something possibly taught from day one.

There is a sense of "You can do anything," of "God can do the impossible," of "You wanna be the first girl to land on the moon? *Go! Go! Be the first girl to land on the moon!*" This coaching chat is important to building people up so they can realize their dreams, but when you subtract what God actually wired someone to do, when you shove His purposes and designs for their existence to the sidelines because you want be as famous as Kathryn Kuhlman, well, heavens, we have a problem. And it's why the world is getting so distressed. The entitlement that comes as a side effect to believing we are special sometimes makes us think we should receive everything on offer, and it's creating disappointments, which leads to anger and negative emotions, which leads to people requiring something to make them feel special. Cue poor choices in relationships, cue buckling at peer pressure, cue addiction, performance mentality, strife.

This heavy desire to make an impact is no bad thing, but it's also coming from the same generation who reportedly are scared to answer the doorbell. "If you're ringing my doorbell, it means IDK [I don't know] you came unannounced and thus gives me no obligation to open my door." Here are two startling revelations in a Twitter thread that went viral.[3] First, *obligation* is a great word for things that the humble don't deliberate over. Second, the words *thus* and *IDK* were used in the same sentence.

We can't be more powerful than the solar system if we are not socially capable of answering the door. We can't be more powerful than the solar system—full stop.

And you need to look no further than Romans 12 to see that this has been an assignment, an attack from the Enemy himself for a very long time. Pride is his favorite subject. How else do you think he got here? It was "pride that changed angels into devils; it is humility that makes men as angels," so Augustine once said.

The truly noble are the truly humble, and they are aware that any gift they have is for serving God and, therefore, others. And within those God-given gifts is a Greek word Paul is referring to, the word *charisma*. The world might define it as having a lively personality or being charming, but Thayer's definition explains it as favor one receives *without any merit of his own*. A divine grace. Grace or gifts denoting extraordinary powers.

This is not something you can acquire or obtain. This is the supernatural, embedded into the very blueprint of personality you were born with. I could practice the piano for ten thousand hours and become a master at it. But I would never play like David Helfgott. Because there is an intrinsic gift, something beyond our own enforced ability, that we cannot and will not create. We cannot, regardless of what we've been told, be "getting on with some charisma." We can work on our craft, but we cannot be the origin of that craft.

My suggestion might be, as we compare ourselves to those we watch from afar, be it in the documentaries, reality TV shows, the Instagrammers who dress their backyards with crocheted hammocks and bouvardia flowers and get paid $100K a week for it, that we can't all be that. We need everyone to take their different roles. To be the church body requires us to be honest about what we are not, as much as what we are. This is the beauty of Christianity; it's not a crutch, it's a glorious co-laboring—a requirement to be more than what you were made of. And you can't do that without each other and without the Lord.

> For as we have many members in one body, but all the members do not have the same function, so we, being many, are one body in Christ, and individually members of one another. Having then gifts differing according to the grace that is given to us, let us use them. (Romans 12:4–6)

The noble know what their gifts are, know what they were wired to do—even if it's tough, even if it doesn't have their name up in lights or beckon their feet to the red carpet. They just get on with it. Because the ego is not allowing itself to be built up with people's approval, nor does it relish praise on its own merit. They are not worried about whether their works will tarnish their reputations or build them. They are too focused on the gifts serving an actual purpose, serving others.

"Influencing the influencers" has become a common phrase in my neck of the woods. And by woods, I mean church. I hear it more from the youngsters than I do from any other generation.

"Did you hear? Did you hear that Jon prayed for Justin Bieber in the toilets at Coachella?!"

"Well, that's nice," I replied. "Any other stories from their time there?"

"No, just that one. *Cool, huh?!*"

I'm not sure if you've ever visited Coachella, but for the sake of my mother reading this, it's a music festival that involves 125,000 hipsters for two weekends in Palm Desert, California. The major issues they face are drugs, perforated eardrums, and a considerable lack of portable toilets. And for the record, JB has a decent entourage praying for him already, so you can understand why I asked this next question.

"I wonder if he prayed for the guy outside the toilets overdosing? Or whether he spoke into the identity of the woman who's been treated like dirt all day because she's just supervising the toilets?"

The noble care about the lost, the poor, the rejected, the outcast, the misunderstood. Not just the famous. Unless the Lord is unequivocally on them. In fact it's the very pull to be around these kinds of famous names that makes us lose influence. The noble care about their craft, their diligence in their work. This, as Proverbs and general life will tell you, always leads us to dine with kings and queens. The point of this proverb was not that we would actually dine with kings and queens; the aim was to inspire diligent work that doesn't desire the delicacies of the banqueting table. And it gives us a warning:

> Do you see a man who excels in his work?
> He will stand before kings;
> He will not stand before unknown men.
> When you sit down to eat with a ruler,
> Consider carefully what is before you;
> And put a knife to your throat
> If you are a man given to appetite.

Do not desire his delicacies,
For they are deceptive food.

(PROVERBS 22:29–23:3)

I once heard a beautiful yet harrowing story that has stayed with me. More than a decade ago, I was talking to a missionary who helped rehabilitate leprosy patients, and she had been working in India. During that time, a Bollywood actress, the next Sophia Loren, the next Marilyn Monroe, was on the rise. She was becoming a household name and starring in many, many films.

She lived with her family until she noticed a patch on her arm. Hiding this for a while, using makeup to cover it, all was manageable until more symptoms presented. Her nervous system was shutting down, and she couldn't feel when she had cut herself or was touching something hot or cold. It was leprosy. So she did what most people afflicted with this disease do and went into hiding. It was bad enough being concerned that she might have already given it to a family member; it was more terrifying that the world might find out that the most beautiful woman in Bollywood was a "leper." It's a term no longer deemed appropriate in today's society, as the stigma has caused such prejudice.

She went into hiding for years, and the family kept her condition quiet from the world. They, too, were frightened of contracting the disease.

Years later, within a hiding area of India, she was found covered in boils, blind, and severely deformed. Because she had been in hiding for so long, the damage was so bad that there was little the hospital could do other than stop the disease from spreading further.

Meeting her at this stage, the missionary asked a rather brave question, one everyone wanted to ask.

"How do you feel living with this deformity from leprosy, when you were, at one point, the most beautiful woman in the country? It must be very harrowing . . . surely?"

There was silence as she sat in the chair looking out the window. The missionary wondered if she had said too much.

"Far from it." She smiled. "My pride would have placed me in very ugly circumstances. In hiding I learned about the soul, our fragilities and how important it is to have them. To care for each other over our own reputation. The praise of others was becoming too much like oxygen for me. I don't believe God gave this to me, but He did turn this nightmare into a noble dream. No, no. I am far more beautiful now than I was then."

Beauty was the only gift she believed she could give to the world. Then in harrowing circumstances, the Lord introduced her to beauty's true meaning and what her real gifts were.

It was a humbling experience even for the missionary. And one that charged all those watching to ask honest questions: *What have I been gifted with? What brings life not just to me, but life to others? What gifts did the Lord give me? Am I using them just for myself? Or am I compensating with some egomaniac lifestyle and limiting my generosity to a modest offering in the Sunday tithe?*

I think the noble, like William Wilberforce, a UK philanthropist who abolished the slave trade, had this humble ethos embroidered onto their hearts. This urgent sense of duty to each other. He was from a prestigious upbringing, wealthy, comfortable. He didn't have to do anything to lead a comfortable existence. But he had an urgent sense of duty to lead the fight to end slavery in England.

I was speaking to an aristocratic friend of mine the other day, when he leaned over and whispered, "Most of them [the aristocracy] are scoundrels. Useless to much of society, rattling around in big houses with vast numbers of alcoholic rendezvous, elements that hindered them from discovering their true gifts. But there are some who are aware that their privilege was actually a responsibility, a duty to the world, to help the poor, to nurse the dying. My grandmother was one. She made it her daily life to read to the blind, or comfort the sick, to pray and donate to those far worse off than she. And it was her faith that got her there; it was her faith that kept mine alive. Privilege wasn't considered an affection from the Lord, as much as it was a quest for duty, for responsibility, to share it with the world."

In this present day of consumerism, we long for more abundance, for all the promises fulfilled. That's part of the kingdom wiring; it's part of understanding heaven in all its abundance, but it mustn't be for our own prestige. Too often we are driven by these as if it will bring us some inner rest, some stillness finally. But where there is more available, there is more turmoil, more to sabotage. Eating disorders, for example, are more prevalent in affluent countries.

Without humility, we won't know how to steward God's abundance, His favor.

Wilberforce had enough money to gamble, and he was actually very good at it, but he gave it up once he saw the effect it had on the people who lost to him. In the nobles' humility, they'll step down if something's causing harm to others, willing to lose if it means the objective of the truth and its kingdom is fulfilled.

They are the greatest peacemakers, the finest negotiators, because without their ego brandishing itself around the room, resolution has a greater force. Wilberforce had to face many defeats, much bullying, much antagonism, before he could make the government see the injustice of the slave trade. He might have been charming, he might have had wealth and influence, but it was his humility that brought the slave's freedom.

Compassion overwhelms the ego and destroys it for good.

And then we look at the all-perfect One. The One who never sinned, who was awesomely flawless, never giving in to the temptations of satisfying the ego in the desert, never trying to appease His critics. The man who didn't deem Himself worthy to be called "good," for that should be placed only on His Father, yet paradoxically was able to accept honor (Luke 18:19). This is the difference between humility and false humility. The truly noble don't lack confidence, nor do they push away kindness or honor from others, because their identity rests on the relationship of an omnipotent God.

I remember the day I distinguished humility and self-criticism. Bill Johnson sat in my office, unaware of my battle. I told him, "I've noticed a connection between hopelessness and self-criticism. But you've always been good with receiving honor, without it igniting the ego."

He smiled for a moment and responded: "If we don't know how to receive honor, we have no crown to place at His feet."

Humility is where true kingship is made. Somewhere between the bowing down to our Lord and the rising up to take the brunt of the hardest tasks is a person who just turned up for duty; and come favor or captivity, come rain or shine, they always know who is really in charge.

There's a piercing reality to this for me. From the time of my advertising days to now, I sensed there was something about dying to the self that bought true liberty. I discovered the hype had no substance, that the praise of others never eased unprocessed pain from the past, that the accolades merely collected more dust, that we had a duty to the livelihoods of others, that I must learn to accept being wrong, that I must be willing to be teachable, no matter how painful it was for my ego. I discovered that the ego didn't care for my well-being, that I was foolish without humility. Only then could I really begin to understand what our Lord was talking about.

How do you carry yourself humbly from the age of twelve to thirty, knowing you are the Son of God? How do you learn to change the world? How could the man who walked humbly, the man who inspired the Wilberforces to follow suit, do so with so much charisma? He simply obeyed, He followed the line of duty, and within His humility He didn't just cause a stir, as we tried to in the boardrooms. He cast out demons, He cleansed lepers, He healed the sick, He raised the dead. If you've ever been a witness to praying for someone with cancer using always the mighty power of Jesus' name and seen a tumor burst right in front of your eyes, you'll know that it's the most humbling thing you can ever witness. Right there, in the moments completely out of our control, comes the most divine, inexplicable power.

Something more powerful than the solar system.

In our humility, we choose to follow the wisdom of God's glory. We choose to listen to His advice, rather than make a cocktail of choices to fit our own desires. We obey even if it doesn't feed the ego, especially if it doesn't feed the ego. And in radical obedience to truth, to Christ, the noble find the miracles. No better scripture enforces this sentiment than John the Baptist's words: "Repent, for the kingdom of heaven is at hand!" (Matthew 3:2).

Over time, in pursuit of nobility, you realize influence starts with God and stops with God. You understand that self-promotion is a pointless task that exhausts us. Self-adoration is emptier than Christ's tomb. And like Christ in His thirty years before His ministry began, you observe. You watch people. You work with excellence on the job you've been given, no matter how insignificant the world may find it. Because it's in the serving where we build trust, and in the trust people begin to listen. Before Christ's ministry, records state that people would travel far for His carpentry, so diligent He was at the humblest of tasks.

Just because we are utterly, zealously loved by the Lord, we should never permit entitlement, "For even the Son of Man came not to be served but to serve and to give his life as a ransom for many" (Matthew 20:28 NLT).

So let's quit the tantrums about what is or what isn't our ministry. Let's stop demanding bean bags and free food for the office because we want a better life. Desist in chasing hashtags just to get more followers and start trusting the fact that the influential already have a pastor praying for them at Coachella. Wisdom will remind you that the forgotten are right outside, their hearts are seeking to be rescued, if only we would listen to the screams of others instead of our own egos.

The Son of God, the sight of whom would make us fall to the floor, the One whose sandals we're not worthy of tying, the One we unknowingly hurt over and over, the One who chased us in the darkest hour, the One who forgave us over and over for the repetitive mistakes we didn't mean to make, "first prepared himself to save the world, by serving in a home."[4]

There is nothing more divinely attractive than the honest reflection of our mistakes. It should be us, the church, inspiring the world with redemption stories by stooping low, instead, it was Joaquin Phoenix accepting his Oscar that made the entire world stop and think, if just for a minute.

> I have been a scoundrel all my life. I've been selfish. I've been cruel at times, hard to work with, and I'm grateful that so many of you in this room have given me a second chance.
>
> I think that's when we're at our best: when we support each other. Not when we cancel each other out for our past

mistakes, but when we help each other to grow. When we educate each other; when we guide each other to redemption.

When he was 17, my brother [River] wrote this lyric. He said: "run to the rescue with love and peace will follow."[5]

We learn in a moment that being honest about our mistakes is not as degrading as we might think. If anything, it's inspiring to learn from the wounds we've inflicted on ourselves and each other.

So let's give each other a second chance. Apologize to your father, make room for your mother's correction, fight for your siblings against your own pride, pass the credit to your coworker, keep no accounts—never mind short accounts, because the ego feeds on that stuff and stops you from meeting the original design of you, the one created and written before you set foot on the earth.

Answer the doorbell, ask how the neighbor's day is, know your neighbor's name, never rejoice in your winning if it caused a mighty blow to the opponent, work more diligently than the job description requires, stoke the fire, stack the chairs, find the need and fulfill it whenever you can with the gifts you've been given. Know that humility is one of the strongest traits of noble character—of one who is willing to be forgotten on this earth so they might be remembered in heaven.

The first martyr of the church, Stephen, began his entire story by collecting the offering of the kuppah basket for the outcast widows of his time. All great tales start with a humble beginning.

Serve at home first, and without noticing, you'll probably save the world.

Now if you'll excuse me, someone just rang the doorbell.

FOR SELF-REFLECTION

Humility can only occur when our identity is set on God's affections.

Answer the doorbell.

The noble reach out to strangers and never see it as an obligation.

Whenever we let the ego have a voice, we are not teachable.

Ask what are the gifts, the charisma you've been given, and learn to play your part, however small.

It is not about the desire to be famous, but the diligence to work on our own crafts.

Entitlement inhibits growth. Even if it's painful, understand those correcting you are wishing to help you.

If Christ came to serve, then so must we, and see a joy, an excitement over the fruits this serving can bring.

Humility invites the miraculous.

With humility, we can steward more responsibility, for we will not sabotage that which we know is not ours.

Humility builds more trust than any other virtue.

Are there areas in your life that you struggle to admit you are wrong in?

Are you kind to yourself? Merciful when you have made a mistake? Are you able to make the distinction between condemnation and conviction?

How do you receive honor? How do you give honor to others?

Are you intentional with allowing others to be a part of your journey? Are you humble enough to seek wisdom?

FROM HUMILITY TO SELF-SACRIFICE

And as it appears, in tales as old as Scripture, humility requires a sacrifice at every juncture, a cost in every ounce of love given. Humility consists of sacrifice at every turn.

"For you, brethren, have been called to liberty; only do you not use liberty as an opportunity for the flesh, but through love serve one another."
—GALATIANS 5:13

CHAPTER 6

DIE TRYIN'

SELF-SACRIFICE

I try to imagine the scene and realize that my imagination will place limitations on the reality of God's majesty. Five thousand people in one spot and a little boy with a big idea. The dilemma of ensuring everyone had food must have been overwhelming for the disciples. This wasn't a stadium event with months of planning involved. Billy Graham had it much easier. There were no food trucks, no Uber Eats. So the sheer adorableness of a young boy thinking that sharing his lunch would help feed the five thousand must have been heart-melting, if somewhat comical.

Of course it wasn't an ordinary gathering; nothing ever was when the Messiah was involved. And as this young boy sacrificed his lunch for the sake of the five thousand others, Andrew, the one it is said was the most approachable of the disciples, saw an opportunity. For with God anything is possible. And so Andrew handed over the fish and loaves to Jesus and observed

His next move. In handing out the boy's food, multiplication instantly began, feeding every person, one by one, fish and bread. Could there be anything more breathtaking? More faith building than this? A God who could wipe out famine in one prayer. A spectacle to show us how heaven truly can invade earth, if only we partner with Him.[1]

Such a simple sacrifice invited an epic miracle, one that nourished not only the family sitting next to the boy, but the entire crowd and with plenty to spare. Who exactly were this boy's parents? How did they raise him to offer his lunch like this? Because apparently the first word I learned after my first day at nursery school was *mine*.

If we learn anything from this incredible story, we know that the subtlest sacrifices are often followed by the miraculous, and sacrifice is something the noble do so well. Whether it's giving up a tuna sandwich or choosing to die for your country, sacrifice comes in many forms: the surrender of our time, our reputation, our fears, our pride, our comfort, our own desires.

This is where, above any other human choice, I witness the presence of the Lord the most. His delight is exuberant in what Jesus confessed: "Greater love has no one than this, than to lay down one's life for his friends" (John 15:13). We can take this literally, saluting the veterans who lost their todays in order to save our tomorrows. The world wars recruited entire generations to save us from the oppression of dictatorship, when the same generations faced knocks on the doors from messengers and telegrams carrying ill-fated news. There is a reason why those who lived through World War II are still considered the Greatest Generation. Many of these truly noble ones aren't around to thank today.

Although we are fortunate enough to face a very different climate today, there are still sacrifices on offer, actions we could take, if only we understood the beauty that would come from paying the costs. I remember how obsessed I was with playing The Game of Life board game, how it was really just a case of going to university, getting a husband, having a couple of kids, getting the first house, then the bigger home, getting promotions, and avoiding as much trouble as possible. The dream, right? But when I look at the people who have inspired me, I see no comfort of the sort. Yes, the family, the children, the jobs speak to our basic needs, but there is so much more need for sacrifice beyond our pleasures—more opportunity for the miraculous to happen.

There are times when our best isn't actually enough, and sometimes we must do what is required. We might sing in praise to God, "Do what You want with me." We might hide in the prayer closets and under deep conviction declare, "I am all Yours and will do anything for You." We might preach to our neighbor and tell them the power of salvation, but there's more. I was so thankful that a friend, bringing thirty people to be saved during an altar call one night, paused and gave them a heads-up about the cost of being a Christian. "I need you to know, this is real commitment. This isn't your get-out-of-jail-free card. This is serious, life-altering, gonna-cost-you-quite-a-bit-of-sacrifice stuff."

But when you're truly in love, when you're head over heels intoxicated by His magnificence, it's game on, baby. And I'm grateful to be surrounded by friends who don't just do their best but are willing to die for the sake of His kingdom come. Their stories are wonderfully wild and full of nobility.

"We are your bullet sponges," a bodyguard said to a friend of mine who was campaigning against the sex-trafficking industry. She was rescuing girls, and naturally the pimps didn't like it. I was stunned to hear the bodyguards share so candidly about how they intended to protect her from bullets by placing themselves in the transport to the base camp, traveling through the most dangerous area of a third-world nation.

Another friend shared how she stacked chairs and furniture against a bolted door in a hotel room in Cambodia so no one could enter her room to kill her that night and destroy her efforts to abolish sex-trafficking rings.

In a different form of sacrifice, a male friend chose a life-time commitment of celibacy because he felt called to lead a fully focused vocation for the Lord, but the commitment didn't come with no sex drive or no desire; he wants to be in an intimate relationship as much as I do. I've not known of many people who pour themselves out the way he does or make such an impact on the care of the souls of others. And a side story—something heart wrenching—is that his mother was waiting to abort him in a clinic forty-four years ago, and something told her to make the sacrifice and keep the child. The way he affects my community today is breathtaking. He has no house to his name, no accolade to introduce him; he's just a father to us and someone we can't imagine living without.

You have the wealthy who give 50 percent or more of their money away. It's why I like noble people to be rich, because then they have more to give away! But it's still a chosen sacrifice. Speaking of financial costs, I have students who spend a year away from working on their own careers and dreams just to help serve my own little vision in California, teaching to many, pastoring pastors, coaching broken hearts, and finding opportunities to heal wherever we go. I have single friends, both men and women, who see a need for more foster caregivers, for more adoptive families, and so give up their fun little solo lives to nurture a child. Their concerns about choosing a child and inhibiting their chances of marriage are given back to the Lord, a worry that can deal with itself tomorrow.

When we served food at the Bowery Mission homeless shelter in New York City, the men were told they had to wear beard nets. You should have seen their faces. They understood the kitchen requirements for the head hair, but not the facial hair. A couple of students began to complain, saying how stupid they felt. Suited up in my own hair net, I smiled, and said, "Let it cost you something." Albeit a minor sacrifice in the realm of vanity, it was a lesson to check the attitude, to check the amusement over it all. After that, they relished the choice, and I found it pretty hard to take the stupid things away from them.

As we take up the invite to sacrifice in the smallest of tasks, the closer we get to God's magnificent love, His breathtaking character. One thousand homeless people were fed that day in New York City. And in our risk of praying for multiplication for more food donations, an eighteen-wheeler turned up completely filled with donations from the finest food brands. By the end of the day, we had so much food we didn't know what to do. That mission risks every day to sacrifice their time just so they can witness another miracle and add a light of hope. And when it hits a code blue, when the temperature in New York falls to thirty-two degrees Fahrenheit or below, they come to sleep in the shelter. It costs time, pride (we'd rather say we work on Wall Street, no?), energy, and the fight against the self to not lose hope.

Acts of nobility come with a price tag. For the sake of truth, the noble lose friendships, families, jobs. They endure not eating, derision, jail, isolation, and sometimes give their own lives. Genocide is a reality Christians cannot afford to ignore today. I am an only child with a widowed mother, and I remember us having a hypothetical conversation. I asked, "If I am to be faced with an AK-47 to my head, if I am told to spit on the face of Christ or choose to die—like those stories you've heard in Korean tribal communities, do we take the stand?"

My mother, without a missing beat, replied, "Yes, we take the stand. I would trust that the Lord would take care of you, if it were to be me, and that you would be faced with such a sense of wonderous awe from above, you'll not notice the pain, like Stephen." It was a powerful moment and the presence of the Lord was tangible. I hope and pray that we never face such a situation, but when it comes to sacrifice, when I've promised Him how I would do anything for Him, I meant it. At least I began to mean it some time in my thirties. Before then, it was empty words that sounded pleasant in prayer.

These choices can be prepared sacrifices like the conversation with my mother or with William Wilberforce's sacrificial attempts to abolish the slave trade. It took twenty calculated years before he saw breakthrough. But then there are the scenarios you can't prepare for, the on-the-cusp moments that will really test the intrinsic wiring of the soul.

Take the case of Father Alec Reid.

In 1988, two British Army corporals, despite being advised to take alternative routes, drove mistakenly into an Irish Republican Army (IRA) funeral cortège in Belfast, Northern Ireland. Just three days before this event, loyalists had boycotted another IRA funeral, opening fire on the mourning crowds, killing three people and wounding sixty. After the horror that had occurred, in the violent climate in Northern Ireland, the tension was particularly high and bitterness was as solid as the brick houses that lined the streets of Belfast.

Father Alec Reid was taking the funeral this day, although I doubt he knew the raw evil lurking around the corner. The two corporals had attempted to drive down back alleys, avoiding the cortège, but after dead ends and blocked roads, they returned back toward the procession and rode on the pavement, causing instant fear that this was another attack from the loyalists.

Crowds surrounded their car and a storm of anger erupted, as Corporal Wood, driving the vehicle, pulled out a gun and fired it into the air. The crowd dispersed for a moment to cover themselves from the gun fire, then the crowds and members of the IRA returned back to the car, dragging out the two soldiers and pulling them along the ground, kicking and beating them in the streets past journalists who later commented on their "terrified eyes."

Barely conscious, they were then dragged to a nearby playground, where they were searched. Captors found military ID on one of the corporals, which was marked "Herford," the site of a British military base in Germany, but it is believed they misread it as "Hereford," the headquarters of the British Special Air Service, the SAS, who were the enemies of the IRA at this time. It was this misreading that led the IRA to not just torture them but to kill them.

Helicopters swirled above; journalists were recording the entire thing (at least the ones whose film hadn't been taken by the IRA), yet no one was saving them. The corporals were silent and never fought back. Father Alec Reid rushed in, trying to protect the soldiers from being shot, even though, technically these soldiers represented his church's enemy. Reid was heaved away by the IRA gunmen and warned that if he resisted, they would shoot him too.

After Reid's removal, the corporals were stabbed, shot, and left barely clothed in the wasteland. The men who murdered the corporals fled as Father Reid ran back to their bodies, noticing one was still breathing. He attempted to resuscitate the gravely wounded man and give CPR, his lips covered in their blood. On failing to revive them, he prayed and read them their last rites. This moment was captured in an iconic photograph of the most turbulent times in the war between the Catholics and the

Protestants. A stark reminder that someone, albeit alone in his perspective, could see what the Lord wept over.

Such sacrifice, to risk one's life in the name of justice, in the name of truth, to read the last rites over the Enemy, was a story that gripped the world. The photograph by David Cairns was later claimed by *Life* magazine to be one of the best pictures taken in the last fifty years. I don't think it was the picture that blew us away as much as the sacrifice and compassion captured through a Canon lens.

Two decades later, Reid took on a role considered "absolutely critical" to the Northern Ireland Peace Process. He wasn't picking a fight; he was choosing the most potent posture, which the religious sectarianism had forgotten—peace. He became known as the "Padre of Peace." But one startling point of this story was that if the IRA had searched Reid's pockets the day of the corporal killings, they'd have found secret documents that were part of an exchange of papers between representatives of the main political parties, Sinn Fein and SDLP (the Social Democratic and Labour Party), as part of a fledgling peace process this priest was trying to facilitate. Documents that Reid knew, if discovered by the IRA, could have cost him his life.

Behind triumphant choices are people passionately running to redeem, restore, and reform that which brings tears to the eyes of the One we love.

As followers of an all-redeeming Lord, we cannot just delight in what He delights in, but we must grieve what He grieves and fight in whichever way wisdom guides us. The noble, in their nonviolence, choose (from a worldview) the "weakest" of weapons: the knee bent to the ground, a refusal of food, a prayer for the dying, a towel with which to wash Judas's feet. Such ammunition is considered to be the most violent for the kingdom, and only the strongest remember to use it when faced with such adversity. Oh, how the toughest minds can sacrifice in the most extraordinary circumstances.

This is where you can tell choices do not descend from ego. They are not for the faint hearted, martyr-wannabes who long for the buzz of significance. Truly sacrificial people focus on the greater good of another. This is the opposite of antagonism gone wild; this is the very art of self-sacrifice, which often comes at short notice, to stay loyal to truth instead of being swayed by fear or by ego.

Why is self-sacrifice one of the elements of nobility?

Because it's the epitome of love, and love without sacrifice is merely a one-way exchange; if it doesn't cost something, is it really love? It is the epicenter of nobility, the focal point of John's gospel, reflected in its most brutal form on the cross. Put bluntly, love is not love at all without sacrifice. Any reticent attitude toward sacrificing for another is like pride, and we all become acutely aware that pride must die in us, else nothing of heaven can live in us.

There is no quicker entry point for heaven to invade our lives than for it to witness our sacrifice and our witness to His. For sacrifice to be given a space to show up and impact not just a moment, but like Father Reid, an entire nation. This is where we find ironic dissonance with the generations to come: they wish to impact the world, but without sacrifice, and if we are asked to sacrifice, to stretch our capacity, to go above and beyond, we complain or act entitled.

The noble are willing to give up their own desires, their own time, their own comfort, their own pride, their own freedom for the sake of another. And they can be found in the humble churches of just thirty members, made up of ones who will never be known or given the Victoria Cross or the Purple Heart. We tend to place sacrifice only on the battlefield, but there are many additional forms of sacrifice available to us, forms I know I've ignored.

Why do we ignore those nudges from the Holy Spirit to stand up for the honorable? For heaven to invade earth? Why do we leave this for others we deem more courageous and tougher than us?

Perhaps it's fear, people pleasing, apathy, detachment, numbing of our own feelings and therefore abolishing any compassion for others, or an inability to experience any more pain than the stuff we haven't processed with the Lord. Or worse yet, perhaps no one has told us the benefits of self-sacrifice, that we get to experience His presence on a whole different level.

In my pastoring journey, I've discovered that the more healed people are, the more sacrificial they become. This desire to fill voids, to minister to one's own pain, to seek relationships that fix an insecurity or need in us, never leaves room for other people, for true love. We might complain about the fact that people aren't helping others, but we need to start asking why. People may be dealing with pain, a need to comfort the self so much that they have forgotten the power of sacrifice.

And it's easy to disconnect with the tales I've just shared and believe we're unlikely to face such violent circumstances in our own lives. But most of our days offer us subtle choices to take a stand in the name of probity, lest we hide in the shadows, watching life as if it weren't to be played with.

I've witnessed a friend get pummeled by bullies in the playground, while I stared on. I've kept silent when my boss was belittled by a television studio because of his eschatological leanings. I've partnered with gossip. I have lost count of the times I should have done the right thing but settled for the wrong. I opted for the poorer choice in favor of a smile and acceptance. I've taken sides—the wrong ones. I have hundreds of unpublished articles hidden in folders, not presented for fear that such opinions would lose me readers. Any opportunity to be noble was jilted for selfish gain or because I didn't trust in the Lord.

Are we willing to brace the beast of people pleasing, of ego stroking, of conforming to the crowd in the name of peace, of justice, of the humility taking the higher road? Can we withstand such remonstration even if it's from those we love? Character influences our choices; choices influence the world around us. Even if we stay silent, shying away from any destined calling, we have still made a point through our nonactions. It takes courage to change hearts. And it's the tenacious pioneers who are usually the lonely ones who take our breath away. Noble archetypes such as these are necessary to challenge culture, to bring justice. Jordan B. Peterson, a professor and clinical psychologist from Ontario, once explained that great leaders are not always "agreeable." They are willing to stand against the tides of society.

As Christians we follow the man who sacrificed so much more than His own life. I don't believe those who have a close relationship with God are ever scared of death. Dying perhaps. The pain of it, without question. But fear of the hereafter is never an issue for them.

On the precipice of courageous acts, we can offer a living sacrifice of our thankfulness in our tiny actions. As Winston Churchill once said, "Character may be manifested in the great moments, but it is made in the small ones."

And with these tests of when to stand up for the lost, the broken, the outcast, or integrity itself, strength and endurance are built in the humble beginnings of everyday choices. Such building then equates to bolder triumphs on the expeditions of life.

If it's not our lives we are sacrificing, it could be our reputations we are willing to place on the line. A notoriety that Christ gave little time for. A concept that other people of influence try to follow suit on centuries later.

In 1991, three years after the corporal killings occurred in Belfast, Princess Diana stood in a leprosy hospital ward in

Nepal, waiting to see the sufferers of what Mother Teresa called "the loneliest disease in the world." It was a scandalous affair for many; after all, it wasn't the "done thing" to allow one's Chanel buttons to mix with boils and bacterium. Her own aides and security had warned her of such a visit.

Now the gravitas of this provocative act must not be ignored. This was radical. Even the missionaries and medical staff, the ones who touch and minister to leprosy patients every day, were astonished that one considered so untouchable herself would take such a risk. Did she know what she was suggesting? A member of the British monarchy and descendant of the British Empire that once ruled India want to meet with leprosy patients? A public declaration to say they are worthy of being spoken to, never mind interrupting her heavily scheduled trip for.

The frenzy from the paparazzi became insipid, as they embarrassingly shouted at doctors to move out of the way. It didn't deter her, and true to tactical form, she did something no one was expecting. She did the unspeakable . . . and took off her gloves.

Making a beeline for the first bed, onlookers thought they'd see a nod, a token sentence of kindness, just a walk-through. No touching, they thought.

She extended her hands to the first leprosy patient. Exchanging her prestige for his compassion. If walls could gasp, they would have. The patient's eyes filled with tears, for she was the first person, outside of the medical staff, to touch him for more than a decade. The second bed held a patient blinded by the disease. His numb stumps could not feel her hand. She felt his face, and it was then that he could finally sense her touch. The only real noise you could hear were the shutters of the cameras going at speeds quicker than an Alexander McQueen show; the rest was stunned silence.

Even though there were just twelve patients in the ward,

the entire continent, if not the planet, was about to know about this. Sweeping through the ward was a fragrance only those who sought Glory would understand. This is what happens in noble moments; I've seen it more than once and felt it a thousand times. Even when this story was first retold to me, the presence of His delight was too intoxicating to miss.

You see, when people remove their fear, a glorious compassion takes over. And in such, an act of nobility takes place. An act that, in this instance, the palace considered a formidable risk, but a kingdom far greater than any monarchy began to fill the crumbling concrete ward.

On that day, sufferers of the loneliest disease in the world were reminded they still mattered to the world. To the regal.

All from just one handshake, one touch, one moment of nobility.

But it was the next day when the monarchy really felt the backlash.

"DON'T DO IT, DI!" screamed the front covers of the press. Flooding the newsstands was the picture, the one she fully expected to be converted to ink and recycled paper within twenty-four hours.

This stirred up social embarrassments at levels not easily plumbed.

This justice move to include the outcast was down to a long-term grievance of her own, something she had experienced herself in very different ways. And what better way to resolve your own pain than by helping that of another?

Despite the controversy, for ten minutes of one intentional action, the "forgotten disease" had been placed into the spotlight again.

That same day Kensington Palace received a phone call: "Hello, sir, I am Tony Lloyd, the director of the Leprosy

Mission, and I wanted to pass on a message if I may to Her Royal Highness?"

"Yes?" The private secretary replied.

"I wanted to say . . . well, I wanted to thank her . . . what she has done in five minutes . . . well . . . we've been trying to do for 120 years. Dispelling the stigma, and making it abundantly clear that leprosy is not as contagious as the world might think."

"Would you mind holding on for a few moments, Mr. Lloyd?"

"Oh. Yes. Absolutely."

After a fairly lengthy silence, a voice came back on the line.

"Mr. Lloyd?" The secretary returned to the phone.

"Yes, sir."

"Would you mind saying that last sentence one more time?"

"Which one? The one about what she had done in five minutes we have been trying to accomplish in 120 years?"

"Tony. I love the work you are doing over there." Either the press secretary had stubbed his toe on a bureau and his voice had increased several octaves higher, or that sounded uncannily like Princess Diana.

"Ma'am?"

"Yes, it's me. What can I do to help you further?"

"Well, I—er—I guess. If it's not too much of a bother. And if you'd like to . . . you could be our patron?"

And from an unpopular decision to shake the hands of leprosy patients, Diana became the greatest spokesperson against the stigma of leprosy in the twenty-first century. Sufferers came out of hiding. Families reconciled. Millions of pounds were funded toward more rehabilitation centers, where patients were given jobs.

In order to actuate nobility, to step into greatness, there must be a mightier motivation than simply being a hero. In fact, I strongly advise against it. Such a longing will not get us through the long haul. We would cave under the pressure—be it from the threat of death, or isolation, or foolishness.

It had been a long time since Diana had wanted to be adored by the people. Nothing deters you more from the need of a standing ovation than when you've already been mocked by enough numbers to fill a stadium. Her friends sold their stories about her for a quick buck. Paparazzi uttered the most gruesome lines under their breath while she walked down the street in order to get that "tearful" photo. No one wants to hear the words "I'm glad your dad died." She had learned by now, on extreme levels, that living off the fumes of people's praise would mean you could die from their criticism. Alternatively, she focused on the truth and what she could do with the influence she had.

Instead of taking so much time to grieve our own pain, taking a stand against another's injustice creates beauty from the ashes. It eradicates a temptation to be introspective instead of useful. To stand against that which hurts our own souls invites a collaborating strength with the Lord.

Some choices changed history, some inspire our neighbor, and some merely build our own character. We mustn't look for the greater impact; we mustn't dream in numbers. Instead we must dream in character, in realms beyond our limitations. What would be our noble choice? Is my choice motivated by fear, a lack of trust in a mightier God, or worse yet, do I wince due to the pride of my own ego?

It is here that Christians could truly deliver the gospel—not by words but by action.

Nobility starts with a heart posture, a planned posture. As Isaiah said, "The noble man devises noble plans; and by noble plans he stands" (32:8 NASB).[2]

And behind it is the motivation for why we stand. It cannot be in heroic tales, but in following the harmonies that heaven rests on. To stand up for all the fruits of the Spirit. To see the darkness and know that we could bring light, if only we chose to. It's not just for the hideous injustices of the apartheid or the prejudices of racial segregation. By standing, we may lose more friends, even our jobs—but we'll never lose sleep.

In valuing this concept of nobility, in small steps, you could tell my character was changing, because my actions began to change.

I stepped in when I saw a man viciously hit a woman. I spoke up when my boss was criticized in a television studio. I asked the gossiper if they had spoken to the person they were talking about—they hadn't. So I did. I started to do the right thing, refusing the inner disquiet of the wrong. I chose the right side, even if it was lonelier. But believe me, heaven's celebration never feels lonely. I've presented articles that caused a lot of controversy, and yes, they lost me readers, but they gave new options to those wanting to find kingdom-minded freedom. Any option to sacrifice was now a privilege, and I was thankful for the opportunities that sweetly knocked on my door. I jilted the selfish option because I finally trusted in the Lord.

When we face great opposition, the Lord gives us greater responsibilities because of the small stepping-stones that write noble endings instead of treacherous or bitter finales. When you're in love, you're all in. There is no negotiation, no balancing act. Nobility is the most unreasonable but rational existence a Christian can walk in. We may not have it all together, and we are never perfect, nor should we strive for perfection over excellence; but there is an encounter waiting on the other side of self-sacrifice. And even if we are not as wealthy in influence as a Billy Graham or as set up as Father Reid, we will be faced with options to sacrifice. And, despite what the world tells us, it's here we find life.

"For whoever wants to save their life will lose it, but whoever loses their life for me will find it" (Matthew 16:25 NIV).

And I don't know about you, but if sacrifice brings the lost home, sees the outcast celebrated, results in a nation of peace, and sees the homeless fed. If not holding onto the reins of my life as tightly invites more glorious surprises, if I get to see miracles upon miracles because I gave up my own desire, if it means I get closer to His affections, to His presence in every room, then I'm willing to die tryin'.

Are you?

FOR SELF-REFLECTION

Nobility must involve sacrifice, for true love cannot occur without it.

If we are in pain, we must find others in the same position and not wait to be fully healed before sacrificing for others. It is exactly this posture that Christ seeks for us to understand.

This is not about being the hero or martyr, for self-promotion or an agenda for self-gain are always caught out in the end.

Sacrifice comes in many forms—from losing your life on the battlefield to risking your own reputation.

We must trust that the Lord will show up in all sacrificial risks.

Let what the Lord grieves over be the motivation to sacrifice.

The cross is the ultimate sacrifice. In every opportunity to sacrifice, let it be a moment to reflect Christ's courage in His own crucifixion.

Does your sacrifice bring great results for others? Ensure that the sacrifice is motivated by an act of love, and not revenge, bitterness, or pain.

Self-sacrifice and the art of choosing to die can only come about in one way, and that is with courage.

FROM SELF-SACRIFICE TO COURAGE

Sacrifice cannot be adhered to repeatedly
without courage. It's from here where
we can love, and love again.

When I am afraid, I put my trust in you.
In God, whose word I praise—
in God, I trust and am not afraid.
What can mere mortals do to me?
—PSALM 56:3–4 NIV

CHAPTER 7

THE BITTER TASTE OF VANILLA

COURAGE

S he had been on the run for three days. She was fifteen and my newfound hero.

She had not chosen to be taken hostage by terrorists—no one ever does—nor had she been asked to witness her school-mates face beatings and rapes, but these were the cards they had been dealt, and escape was her only option. By day three on the run, she came across a tribe who surrounded her. Noticing the crucifix around her neck, they placed an AK-47 to her head and told her to deny Christ. She point-blank (pun intended) refused. So stunned were the gunmen at her sheer audacity, they lowered the guns and let her keep running. Perhaps it was just survival instinct; perhaps she was running out of options. Perhaps she'd prefer to be shot than beaten or kept in captivity again, but not many would have stood in that situation with their head held high, unless they truly believed in what they were standing for.

I was flown out to meet with her only months after her escape. She was finally on a different continent, protected by guards and safe from being hunted down. She retold the entire story comfortably over milk and biscuits. I bought her *Mary Poppins* on DVD, portraying a place that was a far cry from the home she once lived in. She didn't know how to use deodorant; she hadn't seen a duvet cover or water from a tap. Yet there was little trauma, and when she did encounter horrors, she faced them, head on, a type of faith that only the noble seem to achieve. A tenacity that makes me ask what they are taking, and if I can consume a crate of it. And when it came to watching her run track, well, she was breaking school records; Eric Liddell had a run for his money. She wasn't naturally born tough, born fast, but with God's guidance, she learned to have a tough mind and take a stoic stand against those who came between her and her only constant—Christ.

The noble teach us that courage is the mastery of fear, not the avoidance of fear. For we are not in heaven yet, and we have jobs to do, intimidation to conquer, injustice to fight, walls to break down, love to commit, and within all of that, we shall face the many hurdles the Enemy will want to throw our way.

This is more than perseverance. This is a trust that goes beyond. When I was an atheist, it was the scared Christians who made their faith so unappealing. Some hid behind their religion, which made me wonder if the true character of the apostles from the early church had been forgotten. I met ones who dared not play secular music, who were concerned to mix with unbelievers or let their children go to a state school. So much fear, such little resistance to the Enemy. The dude was having a field day while the ones with true authority hid behind the pews. I would read of the apostles, of them rejoicing in their wounds, in being considered worthy of such persecution—oh, the privilege to be counted as one of the afflicted!

Something changed when they went from disciples to apostles. They had this gift of authority that Christ left us, this sense of power that could not, and would not, be beaten. Every time they were sent to prison, they escaped, rushing back to the people. For the courageous, the beat goes on.

These apostles were the epitome of the new frontier. They were the noble, the just, and, boy, were they mighty! They knew now what Christ had left them, and as they partnered with the Holy Spirit, lines of bodies would be laid down along Solomon's portico, with Peter merely walking along the expectant people—his shadow casting healing on the lame, the sick, the dying, and the dead. I marvel. I daydream. I long to be an observer of those days. Such power came with a courage to act with integrity, to be true to the faith, steadfast in the face of any threat. They had a breathless resilience that no demoniac, no threat of death could intimidate. They were like the ultimate fighting champions with superpowers and steroids, and I know we want it today. I know we are desperate to see the miracles at this capacity, for it's the manifestation of His ultimate goodness, but, man alive, are we aware of the courage, the cost?

I feel an intense presence as I write. The drama, the chaos, the commotion, the intense expectation of seeing miracle after miracle waiting in line. It was a 100-percent-satisfaction-or-your-faith-back guarantee. No more battling over who was the best disciple; they had the courage to give up the ego and find a whole different power by laying down their own. Tears fall down my face at the prospect of His delighting in the chance to partner with us, because we got out from behind the pew, stood up for what Christ died for, and began to truly face all evil with a terrifying courage. The courage that crucifies cancer, that emulsifies pride, and instantly extinguishes the God complex of the atheist.

I longed to find people who would stand up like these apostles, to prove my stand for atheism wrong, and on occasion I met with the valiant. For the ones I hadn't met, I found books dedicated to their witness.

The nineteenth-century evangelist Mary Slessor had a similar story to my fifteen-year-old hero. But this time the scene was situated at Wishart Church, Scotland. Located amid the slums, the church had a mission to reach the needy and young, but their open-air attempt of evangelistic ministry was opposed by the slum mobs, who threw mud at Slessor at every given opportunity.

> One night a gang that seemed determined to break up the mission surrounded her on the street. The leader swung a weight fastened to the end of a cord closer and closer to her head. She courageously stood her ground and did not flinch even when the weight grazed her forehead. Amazed and impressed, the leader allowed his weapon of intimidation to fall to the ground and exclaimed "She's game, boys!" Out of admiration the entire gang attended her meeting that night, and some of its members continued to do so in the future. The youth who had swung the lead weight was converted and transformed, and he afterward pointed to that occasion as the turning point in his life.[1]

It is the strongest in the room who have the most influence. We need to be fearless to face the darkest parts of humanity so we can introduce the light. And as we see with the courage of people who trust in the Lord, the bravado of the arrogant is thrown off guard. They are mesmerized that nothing can intimidate these witnesses, not even death. Mary Slessor went on to bring peace to tribes in the most violent of countries. Reports of her knitting while the tribes fought over her were true. It kept her calm, but also kept her present. There is something about the nobles' self-conquest when they were young children that affects their bravery in the future. There is something about Jesus' history that triumphs over trying to battle the odds ourselves. Miracles never show up in the latter, only the former.

I, on the other hand, am not like this. Last time I was faced with any physical horror was when I was visiting the London dungeons with some friends. I put on a brave face and told the group that this kind of stuff didn't frighten me. "A walk in the park," I said, flipping back my hair, limping with one leg and barely murmuring "sup" to the guides. Had there been any cameras taking random photos of this "adventure," you'd see me leaning against a wall chewing on some straw, pretending I am never intimidated by amusement charades.

It wasn't until we were in a corridor with zero light and the low humming sounds of what I can only describe as uncannily resembling a distant soundtrack of *Jurassic Park*, when some actor jumped out from behind the wall, wearing a mask similar to Hannibal Lecter's and carrying a fake knife. Without thinking I grabbed my friend Charlie, holding her like an ironing board to block the attack. I screamed so loud everyone covered their ears. When we exited the venue, Charlie exclaimed, alarmed, "I'm sorry, Carrie, but did you just use me as a human shield?" To this very day, she has never forgotten this story. To this day, I've been unable to deny it.

Awful isn't it? In my moment of panic, in my unthinkable

state of fear, I used my friend's body to protect me. And what's worse, as this was nothing but an immersive amusement that we paid ten pounds for, what on earth would I do in a real-life situation? When I'm really facing a choice? It is for this reason alone that the subject of unreasonable courage fascinates me—because I am monumentally lacking in it.

Even if we veer toward the lower end of the scale, with smaller risks, like asking for a miracle, the worst that can happen is the miracle doesn't occur and we see no breakthrough for healing. But then I think, *This person who wants healing came up to the prayer line with expectations, and what if they don't get healed? Will they think I'm not holy enough to be on this prayer line? Will they make a complaint about my poor skill sets in the miracle department?*

Randy Clark was leading a healing conference in Redding, California, a few years ago, where a woman in the crowd had been healed from a minor skin rash and was jumping and celebrating in victory. But my bold and fearless friend Bill wondered if she was struggling with walking. He told her to sit on his seat with her legs out to assess if they were both the same length. It was evident that they were not—there was at least an inch difference in length.

He held onto her feet, looked her straight in the eyes, and said, "Watch this."

After a few words of prayer, her shorter leg began to grow out, not just a little but at Pinocchio-nose speed. It was extraordinary. And right after I screamed at the cartoon likeness of it all, she ran down the aisle cheering, losing all sense of dignity—as we all should at such a moment. I sometimes wonder if the Lord not only wants to establish His original design back into someone's body but expedites the miracle purely for the love of that person's reaction.

However, I was more stumped with Bill's approach. I said, "You see, the difference between you and me, Bill, is that if I'm faced with that kind of request, with a leg that needs to grow, I'll start with a rather low-toned, somber even, 'Let us pray.' I grit my teeth and hope for the best. You, however, Bill, start with 'Watch this.' Talk about high stakes."

Never was the scripture "Now faith is the substance of things hoped for, the evidence of things not seen" more appropriate (Hebrews 11:1). In the natural, we usually seek evidence before we have faith. Before we're courageous, we wait for the inflatable cushion down below to catch our fall. It's called risk management, and it makes millions of dollars for the economy. But when it comes to the kingdom, as radical as it is, it asks us to believe in the evidence of the unseen so we may partner with God, to do the ultimate and believe in His goodness. It's the faith in Him that moves Him. Even with faith as small as a mustard seed, we move the heart of God, and with that He moves the mountain.

I missed the vital middle part, the part where we move the heart of God. I might contend for miracles or choose to be courageous, but years ago it had nothing to do with intimacy. Do we understand that we could perform so much of the gospel without meaning one patch of it? I missed the chapter that said courage had nothing to do with the belief in our own strength, but every belief in His. How it's really all part of our love story with Him. And as much as I'd take a bullet for my mother, why wouldn't I do the same for Him?

Because I avoided risks, the pain of failing, or unanswered prayers, I hid, finding a more anointed pastor to pray for the sick or delegating someone else to have a confronting conversation. I was cocooned in fear. I never owned my fear, nor admitted to it—I was too prideful for that, too fearful of looking fearful.

Besides, no one wants to be called a pansy. But if we do not challenge our inner fears, we lose opportunities to experience His majesty in the most frightening moments.

When Daniel was thrown into the lions' den, he was approximately eighty years old. He wasn't in the prime of his life, for one as old as he, Daniel certainly went into the persecution with a solidarity in trust—no doubt a trust that had built over the years. Daniel is possibly my favorite character in the Bible after Christ, for this reason alone. He never ran; he never made an excuse; he didn't choose to work for kind Christian aid workers or in a cozy little parish in Wensleydale, where the most wicked action to take place in the last forty years was a vandalized post box. He was working for the Stalins, the Hitlers, the evil ones of their time. In private Daniel called for repentance over the city and refused to let anything taint his food, focus, and prayer. His undivided devotion that Paul so wishes we all had was evident in Daniel's daily life, and it's this intimacy that strengthened his trust in God when he most desperately needed it.

Imagine being so praised in one breath by the equivalent of the Illuminati, and then vilified in the next; not only did Daniel face the challenges before him, but he often invited the rebuttals. His first time serving Nebuchadnezzar, he asked to eat only fruit and vegetables; and though the guardians warned him he would not be able to work with such a diet, Daniel essentially uttered "try us" (Daniel 1:13). He fully believed the Lord could maintain his body mass and strength during the fast. Such courage impressed Nebuchadnezzar but also infuriated him. When Daniel faced trials, such as being thrown into the den of lions, there was no flinching, no excuses, no suggestion of someone taking his place; and whenever death knocked at Daniel's door, there was Christ. Every. Single. Time.

Surely every risk we take with our trust in the Lord, every rescue in His mercy builds our history. But if we never take a risk, we never create a history that is accurate to a kingdom mindset. Dens of lions or burning fires, wicked leaders or water fasts need not be the way to build courage, but they are stories that serve as a perfect reminder when we come face-to-face with fear.

There is a connection between purity and power that mustn't be ignored. The more self-control I see in people, the stronger their confidence seems to be—not just in themselves but in their God. There's a reason self-discipline is part of the fruit of the Spirit; we need His strength to keep us focused. The more we build a heart of integrity, the more favor and responsibility will come our way—things that require a huge amount of courage. There is a particular flavor, a certain antiquated taste to this kind of courage. Hitler had received praise for his bravery as a young soldier, but that kind of courage held a rotten smell of orphan spirit and bitterness toward the elite.

No, truly noble fortitude is underlined by a full belief that the world belongs to God and not to the world itself. The customs of this world are fleeting, ruthless even; yet if we follow cultural trends, we can navigate life with ease, comfort, and prosperity. You can understand why two-thirds of the world struggles at times to devote their lives as Christians. They are told that if they choose to follow God, they may expect pain, loss, and unpopularity. But the noble Christian would prefer to lay down the unstable promises of the world for the truth and prosperity of God's kingdom. That's where true courage comes from—a vision after us, a legacy beyond our deathbeds.

Napoleon might have shown great bravery on the battlefield, but Lord Charles Fox in the House of Commons gave an impeccable speech that left the government silent and in awe. It dealt with not just the abolishment of the slave trade, but also the difference between noble gestures for the freedom of another and, therefore, God, as opposed to daring gestures based in our own gumption.

> When people speak of great men, they think of men like Napoleon, men of violence. Rarely do they think of peaceful men. But contrast the reception they will receive when they return home from their battles. Napoleon will arrive with pomp and power, a man who has achieved the very summit of earthly ambition. And yet his dreams will be haunted by the oppressions of war. William Wilberforce, however, will return to his family laying his head on his pillow and remember: the slave trade is no more.[2]

Let there be no question that the noble gain in life what they have the courage to ask for. It isn't always about which doors the Lord has opened for them; it is about which ones are willing to step over the threshold and walk through. This kind of courage, this kind of nobility, is what made me question the atheism I had marinated myself in so many years ago. For nothing, no logical argument, could catch my breath as much as the fearlessness of a devoted Christian. Brother Yun, also known as the Heavenly Man, could survive without bread and water for a record number of days. Even though his wife was unable to identify him in prison, our Lord sustained him. And within that witness, all his fellow prisoners found their own freedom in the salvation they chose under Brother Yun's watch.

Hebrews 11, also known as the Hall of Faith chapter, is a stunning record of God's most beloved and courageous people, the ones who stood the tests of time with unshakable faith. You cannot argue, you cannot find fault in His goodness, when you hear that account of how the courage of all those people listed were the labels to the garment that cloaked His glory.

The sweetness of a Christian is of paramount poignancy, but without the willingness to rest on His strategies, His mission and heart, we become vanilla. Void of substance. Void of anything noteworthy. Like a good idea not carried out by the one who had the revelation, courage will go and find someone else to function through. In short, vanilla becomes not pleasant but bitter to taste. For so much flavor, so much goodness has been avoided, for the sake of our tiny thinking. It's a dead belief with no faith in God showing up today. It's dull. Unimaginative. Pointless.

The names in Hebrews 11 were written for us.

The faith of Abraham, who was called out from his comfort and into the unknown, dwelling in the land of foreign promise; tents were his resting place to wait upon the Lord for real foundations. The faith of Sarah, who conceived at ninety years of age for she had judged Him faithful. And after all this obedience, steps made in courageous sacrifice, and decades of waiting, the Lord asked to have Isaac, their only son. Trusting again, after all this, that should Isaac be sacrificed, God would raise little Isaac from the dead.

Oh, the conversations they must have had on the way to the place Abraham was to sacrifice his child. Oh, the pain, the torment, the guilt of killing your own son—in confusion, in utter despair, after all this waiting, to celebrate the arrival of a son, and then to give him back. But the noble stick to their first love, the commitment they made and the love they trust in the Lord. For Isaac was His as much as Abraham's. An expectation to raise Isaac from death was the only hope. And in the test, our God conceded with thankfulness that Abraham did truly love Him.

And the names keep coming: Moses, "choosing rather to suffer affliction with the people of God than to enjoy the passing pleasures of sin, esteeming the reproach of Christ greater riches than the treasures in Egypt; for he looked to the reward" (vv. 25–26).

Gideon, David, Samuel—"subdued kingdoms, worked righteousness, obtained promises, stopped the mouths of lions, quenched the violence of fire, escaped the edge of the sword, out of weakness were made strong, became valiant in battle, turned to fight the armies of the aliens. Women received their dead raised to life again" (vv. 33–35).

The more I fill my mind and my soul with the stories of the brave, the less I wish to discover the bitter taste of vanilla. The more alive I become with the miraculous over our fear and control. It needn't be only the scenarios you read about in the papers, for the smallest afflictions need a faithful touch.

As I woke this morning, like any other morning, I asked our Lord what a day in the life of the brave looked like.

He answered me, like poetry, as if He dreamed of these moments with His children, as if this really was the most pleasing thing for Him, the gift of courage that rests on the shoulders of His goodness. He said:

> *A day of the brave looks like:*
> *The apology you are able to give.*
> *The workplace you choose to keep showing up to.*
> *The visit to the dentist you've been putting off.*
> *The afflicted you pray for on the street.*
> *The demons you deliver in the middle of an occult-ridden house.*
> *The hard decision to end a codependent relationship.*
> *The perseverance of working on a healthy relationship.*
> *The choice to not settle for comfort.*

The choice to not succumb to perfectionism.

The sexual ethics you decide to stick to, knowing you'll be rejected.

The freedom from pain you're willing to admit you have.

The ownership of vulnerability to someone you truly love.

The childlikeness that's finally being given airtime.

The covering of someone's name when they brutally hurt you.

The capacity you stretch to because you see someone in need.

The person you befriend because he or she inspires you (it's frightening for many).

The people you stay loyal to because you are accountable to their wisdom.

The promotion you accept.

The promotion you give away in favor of the colleague who needs it more.

The yes you gave in a crowd full of no.

The no you gave in a crowd full of yes.

The staying quiet in the face of antagonism.

The speaking up when no one else will.

The love you sow without expectation.

The vision you decided to follow, no matter how terrified this makes you.

The spouse you no longer hide behind.

The child you no longer hide behind.

The job you no longer hide behind.

The freedom you brought to an addict, for you are brave enough to show compassion.

The harder road taken, because you finally trusted Me.

The miracles you begin to record on paper, because you gave Me room to show up.

The sacrifice of My Son for the sake of those who will reject My name.

But, My tiny one, the day you let Me fully into all of your being is the day you become the bravest; it'll be the same day you learn to say, "watch this."

On April Fool's Day 2019, I was praying on the floor of the Resting Place in New Jersey for a lady who must have been in her seventies and had level-ten back pain. She told me of the tears she had cried that morning, begging for this to stop.

A student of mine, Zach, came around to the bottom of her feet, seeing if her legs were aligned. They were 1.5 inches different in length. I looked at Zach, and then looked at the lady. I bent down to her eyes, laid my hand on her neck and said in full belief, "Watch this."

If you're a man or woman of faith, you'll know the ending to her story that night.

A story that started with pain was met with some courage, and ended in a jubilant miracle.

FOR SELF-REFLECTION

Courage has nothing to do with our bravery, but everything to do with our trust in God. Every step of risk with Him builds our historic love story with Him. No feat for the kingdom is ever unmet with support, comfort, and victory.

We need warriors of the faith who are willing to risk it all.

Within the courage of the noble comes a bystander, closer to witnessing Him. He turns the weakest into the bravest.

Courage in its simplest form is unlimited love, without expectation.

What areas in your life do you need to be more courageous in? Where do you need to hand over more trust?

Who do you need to be courageous for?

What areas have you been passionate about but too scared to try? What areas in your life do you need to confront? To seek his wisdom on?

If only we didn't fear pain so much, we might be more courageous in the moment, more loving toward the sinner, and more diligent with the truth.

FROM COURAGE TO WISDOM

Unlike a bull, we do not enter the china shop and obliterate everything in sight just to make a point. We do not use courageous force without wisdom. Unreasonable courage should only be mastered when we are given the green light by Him.

"I consider that our present sufferings are not worth comparing with the glory that will be revealed in us."
—ROMANS 8:18 NIV

CHAPTER 8

SOUTHERN WHITE-FACED OWL

WISDOM

He kept stealing. Reports were coming in from different parts of the school to the housemaster, Mr. Taylor, from the teachers to the dining staff. Bernie, a thirteen-year-old boy, kept stealing food. The school could place him in the bracket of "kleptomaniac" and hold onto their handbags. But the beauty of true wisdom, the sheer audacity of nobility, is that it seeks to understand.

After many reports, the housemaster held back on punishment or retribution for the moment and decided to ask a simple question: Why? The boy solemnly entered the housemaster's office.

"I've been hearing reports, Bernie, that you have been stealing food from the canteen during the breaks. Is this true?"

"Yes, sir."

The housemaster was rather taken aback by Bernie's direct honesty, almost relieved that this meeting was going to be less of a battle than he originally thought.

"But why, Bernie? Are you not given dinner money from your parents?"

"My father gives the money to my stepmother, but she never gives it to me. I don't get to see that money."

As Mr. Taylor probed further, the story unfolded that Bernie's father had remarried a woman only a few years older than Bernie. She was nineteen and jealous of the love and attention his father gave him. So when the father worked long hours and felt he could leave Bernie in the hands of his new wife, little did he know that his son was slowly starving. If she was feeling generous, she would make him a jam sandwich some nights, but other than that, the boy was left to survive alone.

For many months, the boy would go hungry. Stealing chips, apples, and bread was a matter of survival. Still, he didn't want to uncover the family situation. Even if there was money available, it was not getting into the right hands. Moved with compassion, Mr. Taylor set up a deal with Bernie.

"From now on, you won't have to pay for your school dinners and snacks, but in exchange, I'm going to ask that you help the canteen staff by cleaning the tables and washing the dishes."

It was a sweet resolution, and once the story behind Bernie's behavior went back to staff and teachers in the school, the boy became so favored, so loved, the school kids couldn't quite understand why he'd turned from beast to brawn. A conundrum that echoed the heart of the unfair gospel. Behind every generous move toward sinful natures is always an explanation of why they are behaving the way they are. The piteous thing about our society is that so few are wise enough to probe deeper.

Wisdom in this world is different from the wisdom of a noble. It does not count on how quickly you can resolve the riddle of the Rubik's cube or the result of your IQ test. It does not care if you are as talented as Verrio or Tolstoy. It does not necessarily appear in a raucous debate like the one where Ben Shapiro "slayed" another liberal in a convention somewhere in Utah. Kingdom wisdom is not a passive virtue but an active one, something that relies on the perspective of God and does not build its foundation on intellect or experience. Intellectualism does not always equate to heavenly wisdom; history shows us that when Germany voted Hitler into power, it was a country that was at the time considered the most intelligent in the world. And it does not always guide itself by the law of the land, for the slave trade was legal until the humanely divine wisdom of William Wilberforce fought tooth and nail to abolish it.

With noble wisdom, there is a prudence, a practicality, a devotion to the right application of knowledge. It holds a true insight into the nature of things but doesn't restrict itself with the limitations of the law. It looks beyond culture, feelings, popularity. When Mr. Taylor heard of Bernie's food theft, it would have been too easy to have let feelings lead to conclusions. Assumptions truly get the better of us. They have wrecked marriages, dismantled careers, and created incessant amounts of prejudice. The finest leaders hold back on personal conclusions and seek an apostolic view—meaning they are always open to reason, and they always filter the situation through the eyes of compassion.

Many noble virtues reside in the art of holy thinking, to execute decisions that create fruitful outcomes for the entire body of people, not just ourselves. This is an almighty dynamic in the church that, in my humble opinion, is sadly lacking in today's age. Christians have a long history of legalism, backed by doctrine, using limiting language and Scripture in the hope it will change someone else's mind. But Jesus was doing something different. Sinners loved to be with Jesus, a stark comparison to how they might feel with us today. Original thought, anointed by our God, urges us to seek out why that is the case, to change our narrative into something more majestic, yet relative. For without it, we are a dying breed relying on the fumes of yesterday's testimony.

Wisdom is active, intentional, creative; it shows foresight and discerns the very crowd that chooses to watch us with morbid fascination. It comes from a hunger within us, a hunger that longs to understand God before ourselves.

Courage, self-sacrifice, perseverance, charisma may all be vital components of nobility, but divine wisdom must be exercised for nobility to be effective. For any of it to make sense. The book of James contains a beautiful passage defining the difference between worldly wisdom and divine wisdom.

> Who is wise and understanding among you? Let him show good conduct that his works are done in the meekness of wisdom. But if you have bitter envy and self-seeking in your hearts, do not boast and lie against the truth. This wisdom does not descend from above, but is earthly, sensual, demonic. For where envy and self-seeking exist, confusion and every evil thing are there. But the wisdom that is from above is first pure, then peaceable, gentle, willing to yield, full of mercy and good fruits, without partiality and without hypocrisy. (3:13–17)

An entire four-hundred-page thesis could be written on this passage alone. But taking highlights from this concept of heavenly wisdom, note that James attached wisdom with understanding—you cannot have one without the other. The beauty of the story of Mr. Taylor and Bernie was that Bernie's housemaster sought to understand. He omitted the option to have feelings before a conversation. Oh, how often I have been at the brunt of a situation where no one asked questions. On the receiving end of assumptions made by bosses or brothers. They pull away in their own conclusions, scattering into the sunset before I'm able to talk with them, before they've asked me for a truth or two. This meekness that wisdom must reside in begins with questions and ends in compassion. Through this, we seek a wider understanding of how to resolve a problem, how we bring the kingdom into the affair. It is here that we carry out some beautiful applications of pansophy.

We discover that the pastor has had an affair, and overnight we leave his ministry, his patronage, removing all loving relationship, crossing the street if he comes across our path. The same man who was there for us in the loss of a father, or healed our sick aunt, does not have his kindness reciprocated, because we concluded that because of his sin, his lack of wisdom, the best option was to shun him. To show compassion at this stage might condone the terrible mistake this person made. We remove our tithe, warn people of this person's unrighteous character, and before you know it, he's not only heading toward full immersion in shame but runs off to seek more comfort from the worst place to find it—in the arms of the original mistress. Our stupidity, fueled by fear of failure and mess, propels more of theirs. We had a missed opportunity with them, to come closer, just like Christ, to ask why, to seek an understanding. In their own pain, we might find God's wisdom in prayer, in gentle confrontation, in tear-soaked handkerchiefs and countless cups of tea. But those who choose the latter course, are so few, so far between. I say this based on the breakup of churches, of division, of numbers lost and chapels converted into condominiums.

Our lack of wisdom starts not just with our sin, but with misunderstanding another's background, with one slight difference to me—most of these pastors were married in their early twenties. They held quite a bit of wisdom and revelation of the Lord—something very obvious when they spoke. Very few had made any, in religious terms, "major errors," such as sex before marriage, porn addictions, theft, fraud, or involvement in the occult. Their greatest sin was probably being a tad passive when their husbands had forgotten to do a chore last Saturday. Every day we all pastored people through relationships, marriage, and the workplace. Essentially 80 percent of our day is counseling, guiding others closer to the Lord. For this particular panel we were speaking to five hundred ladies on the subject of relationships and sexual ethics. Unlike my fellow colleagues, I was unmarried and far from squeaky clean when it came to my past. I had had sexual relationships and dalliances with men that I wasn't proud of. It took many years to rid myself of the shame (never religious shame—just shame of rejection) and to feel worthy enough to be onstage with these fellow pastors.

I knew the wisdom, I knew the guidelines—what to do and what not to do—but somehow, in certain areas of my life, especially when it came to the one place where dreams had not yet been fulfilled (marriage and children), until a couple of years before this panel I kept choosing ignorant paths. For this panel, I was coming from a very different angle. And it's why I would sometimes find myself having a different perspective of Christ than that of my colleagues; I had to experience a lot more grace and mercy from our Lord than perhaps they did.

One pastor took the microphone to answer a question about making unwise sexual choices. "I don't believe that anyone truly loves Jesus if they sin," she said.

I could feel the convictive weight in the room as the cogs

began to turn in the ladies' minds. All of us had sinned at some point, so did that mean we didn't love our Lord? Did that mean Peter did not love the Lord when he denied Him three times during Christ's arrest? I could see why she was coming from this angle, her own culture reveled in reformation, in the black-and-white rules of restoration; she was a pioneer in breakthrough for people, and she had a gift in getting people to change their ways. But I wasn't sure I agreed this time.

"I think I might think differently," I murmured. I was unable to speak with as much conviction as she had, because she was more "sinless" than me. Her actions spoke louder than mine had in our pasts, so I instantly wanted to cower from the mic and say nothing at all. But for the sake of another girl who was about to disqualify herself from the room and from the intimacy of God, I felt the Lord nudge me to speak.

I went in as gently as I could.

"I'm not sure it's a matter of whether we love Him, but more perhaps a matter of whether we understand Him." For years I didn't understand Him, nor did I understand that I was made in His image. So I chose sin, and still make mistakes—just hopefully not the same ones. I pray that every time I fail, I actually listen to His heart on the matter, that I am willing to hear His truth by ridding myself of any denial, of blame toward another. And in this space, the rest turns to gold. The crowd exhaled, relieved that their entire devotion to the Lord wasn't quantified on how many mistakes they made or how many people they hurt, but that this was a journey to seek more of His face so we would become more and more like Him in wisdom, in kindness, and therefore, in nobility.

My own revelation of wisdom, albeit later in my years than I would have liked, didn't come from the book of James, but from my own shortcomings. I was so often the one who knew all the right answers, but when push came to shove, I chose the option that made me feel better in the moment over being wise, sincere, or full of mercy. I was the hypocrite that James refers to; I just didn't want to take ownership, blaming instead the circumstances I faced or the hurtful choices made by another.

I didn't have enough self-respect—something the nobly wise hold onto so well. When they make decisions, they consider the outcomes, the price of things. In some ways they exhibit a stubborn toughness that doesn't budge on their choices. Such a tactic is usually only affiliated with politicians or headmasters rigid in their opinions. Resilience, however, is necessary to embrace wisdom, one that is built on the firm foundations of faith in God over our own gumption. Or, worse yet, feelings. In Martin Luther King Jr.'s opinion, it's the tough mind and tender heart that can stop society from being prejudiced. That can make them wise.

But if we are so easily swayed, so swept up by the change of the wind, we switch our tune with the turns of culture. We focus on trends instead of the Trinity. On feelings instead of His steadfast character. We put down the gospel as outdated, but the truly wise, the noblest of them all will remind you that the Bible was not written for only its own time but for all humanity. The Bible, which holds the greatest wisdom, wisdom that has been tried and tested for centuries, is not outdated—it's avant-garde.

As I've sought His wisdom in my personal dilemmas, I have often looked for "signs" for the right choice, for the noble way. Don't tell me I'm the only one here—you have thrown down a thousand fleeces like an insecure Gideon too. I've prayed for the river in front of me to part like the Dead Sea, for two porcupines to show up in a row, for the glory cloud to appear near the ATM, for a nonscary visitation from an angel, for a twenty-four-carat gem that turns up on my pillow—anything to show that I am doing the right thing.

In distress, I have clawed at the carpet of my bedroom, crying out to the Father late at night as I fight the battle between my desire to be in love and the advice of everyone telling me he's a bad piece of news for the prosperity of my heart. Knowing too well in my midthirties I was so longing to be married, the affections of men had become too enticing. I was settling for questionable characters and noncommittal whispers of empty nothings. My discernment was always spot on, a gift from the Lord that I so rarely used. I knew I had to pull away from this handsome chap; however, my discernment didn't feel like it was enough (clearly I didn't trust myself) and in my complete vulnerability, I was sure that the Lord could hear my cries, like a wailing Hannah. This was my full truth, and I longed for Him to comfort me in my honesty. I heard nothing from Him that night but knew with the thickness of His presence in my room, He was planning a way to show me His heart.

My flatmate knocked on my bedroom door the next morning. "Have you seen outside the door, Carrie?"

"No? What is it?"

"Come look," she said.

Underneath the first step down from our apartment front door was a tiny gray southern white-faced baby owl. A real one. Live and direct. Sitting quite contently on our threshold. I asked for a sign, and here he was. He sat there, just watching us for twenty minutes. I stayed glued, and in the innocence of this bird I felt the wisdom to trust in His goodness, His heart to have plans to prosper me, to keep me safe in all matters. That anything certain in heaven should not need questioning on earth. To step back from the guy who was not right for me. A live owl, the embodiment of a spiritual animal for wisdom if ever there was one, was camping out on my doorstep at eight in the morning. Wisdom would have taken action, listened to the advice of my counselors, God, and the baby owl.

But the pain of feeling unworthy as a single was too strong, and for most of us, unprocessed pain often spells the end of wise choices. I was looking for a sign for the right decision, when God actually wanted me to understand why this was so complicated in the first place. These requested—or should I say, demanded—signs from God don't necessarily build character, self-trust, or self-respect. If anything, they can stunt us in our growth, a get-out clause that keeps us from building a history of making wise decisions, by trusting Him. And above anything, He loves to help us build character, for it helps us stand the tests of time.

Had I self-respect, had I resolved with forgiveness the bitterness toward past hurts, had I abolished self-seeking with a wider scope for others' needs, wisdom would have come with clarity already. And after the courage to process pain with the Lord, after the ranting to Him must come questions about wisdom; we must seek insight from His perspective.

I might have had a decent IQ, but divine wisdom had nothing to do with that and everything to do with the meekness of honesty, of trusting God's advice, of surrendering to His brilliance.

Statistically, we are more intelligent than people one hundred years ago. IQs have steadily increased, with the average person today being considered a genius compared to someone born in 1919. It's a phenomenon known as the Flynn Effect. This sadly doesn't explain, however, why we are not resolving the world's issues. One researcher observed, "Higher IQs have not brought with them generally satisfying solutions to some of the world's or the country's major problems—rising income disparities, climate change, pollution, organized violence, terrorism, deaths by opi-oid poisoning, among others."[1]

In my very humble opinion, in my novice state of observation, I believe it is compassion that leads us to discover the root issues. Compassion is the digger of dirt, and with it comes a bold clarity for solutions. A virtue that is never celebrated, rarely mentioned, and certainly never referenced in the news. This might also be the reason why politics is in a crisis. Negotiation is a forgotten technique, as is finding resolution in exchange for the ego and slaying with witty quips and popularity polls. You want to know the real world-changers? They're on the missionary frontline, holding the dying, the freedom fighters of the modern age.

Through discipline and learning, Daniel established himself as a wise man, ten times wiser than his peers. His reverence for the Lord and purity of heart established the heavenly wisdom that James teaches. Like power, there is a connection between purity of heart and wisdom. The motives behind the lens invite true foresight to unfold. If we begin with a prideful agenda, if we are filled with bitterness or envy or restricted with our own fear, we will never come up with results that establish His glory in our own plotlines.

One story that I reference when teaching my students to look beyond the obvious is a story about Daniel. It is not found in the book of Daniel, but in the apocryphal records. It depicts to me the beautiful conundrum of people taking stories at face value, while the wise make further investigations into initial false allegations. Daniel had discernment from the Lord and, in his purity, distinguished between integrity and manipulation. The accusers became the accused.

A Hebrew wife named Susanna was falsely incriminated by lecherous voyeurs. As she bathed in her garden, having sent her attendants away, two lustful elders secretly watched her. When she made her way back to her house, they accosted her, threatening to claim that she was meeting a young man in the garden unless she agreed to have sex with them.

She refused to be blackmailed and was arrested. She was about to be put to death for promiscuity when the young Daniel interrupted the proceedings, shouting that the elders should be questioned to prevent the death of an innocent. After being separated, the two men were cross-examined about what they witnessed but disagreed about the tree under which Susanna supposedly met her lover. In the Greek text, the names of the trees cited by the elders form puns with the sentence given by Daniel. The first said they were under a mastic tree, and Daniel said that an angel stood ready to cut it in two. The second said they were under an evergreen oak tree, and Daniel said that an angel stood ready to saw him in two. The great difference in size between a mastic and an oak made the elders' lie plain. The false accusers were put to death, and virtue triumphed.

Heaven must breathe a sigh of relief whenever a lover of our Lord uses divine wisdom. Over and over again, wisdom not only brings the peace that James refers to, but it saves lives. Against the sheer audacity of deception from the elders came Daniel's heroic desire for truth. He was an impartial questioner of the law. The noble are not swayed by the crowd or the illusion placed before them. They probe, until all questions are answered. Again it was Daniel's empathy that brought a wider scope to the scenario.

Second Corinthians 1:3–4 says, "Praise be to the God and Father of our Lord Jesus Christ, the father of compassion and theGod of all comfort, who comforts us in our troubles, so that we can comfort those in any trouble with the comfort we ourselves receive from God" (NIV).

If we experience the truly mind-blowing compassion of our

Lord in our most foolish state, then we will discover His wisdom in our honest pain and find compassion for those who hurt us. In short, let us as a church no longer linger upon what people have done wrong but ask with benevolent hearts why someone acted this way in the first place. Let us sit nobly as friends with them in their darkest hours so that with a helping hand, they may know their truth. There is always reason, always an explanation, and it's divine wisdom that seeks to understand it. It's the curiosity beyond the offense that brings us to individual and corporate world solutions.

Then there is the importance of self-compassion that breeds "good works." As a religious entity, we, the church, are often the hardest on ourselves. The Enemy loves to play and distort conviction with shame, and within that dance comes the foxtrot of self-hatred. A back-and-forth cycle of shame, which leads to perfectionism—and, before we know it, criticism becomes a best friend. It doesn't stop with ourselves; it becomes a brutal commentary on everyone around us. It's here where the wise are wary. For if we note people being critical of others, it means they are critical of themselves. Without a splashing of compassion, we are just the same as the rest of society, warring with words online, thinking we have resolved the world's problems with opinions that merely stay in the digital codings of the Internet and rarely turn to action. The fruit of this rivalry becomes a lack of respect for authority, a lack of honor for each other, and the most unsafe environment for creative thinking, for original thought to breed. *Forbes'* coverage of recent research tells us that self-compassion is the prerequisite to success. You are more likely to succeed if you know how to be kind to yourself.[2]

And being kind to yourself invites the wisdom of others. It invites wisdom from people who do life better than you. Wisdom that you don't only listen to but adhere to. Proverbs tells us that "in the multitude of counselors there is safety" (11:14). We can rely on our trusted committee to create safety for ourselves. We have blind spots, subjective angles, so we must be humble enough for teachability. The most unwise Christians are the most prideful, running from pillar to post, refusing to face the hard critique that could be life changing. To build a sense of self-compassion, we are seeking always to build trust with ourselves, trust with our Lord, and it's why, after my southern white-faced owl experience, I followed the advice of people more fruitful than I in the particular area of my struggle—especially when my feelings want to go one way but the rest of my "committee" said no.

There must be a hunger in us for divine acumen. Age has very little to do with it. Travel might expand the mind, but it doesn't necessarily transform it. A man might travel the world, but he still can hold onto his porn addiction like a kid with candy floss. No number of miles traversed can help you confront your own limitations. Wisdom tells you to stay put and fight the dragon. And it's the renewing of the mind that Paul teaches the Ephesians—to stop excusing their actions based on their former ways of life. For this reason, I'm nervous about our generation. We are so introspective regarding past trauma, the harsh words of a church member, the letdowns of former bosses, the discriminations of our brothers and sisters, we snub the opportunities that wisdom is giving us in the present.

To say yes, to surrender to God's wisdom, is the start of true freedom.

If indeed you have heard Him and have been taught by Him, as the truth is in Jesus: that you put off, concerning your former conduct, the old man which grows corrupt according to the deceitful lusts, and be renewed in the spirit of your mind, and that you put on the new man which was created according to God, in true righteousness and holiness. (Ephesians 4:21–24)

Although we are in the golden age of intelligence, according to some sources, wisdom is actually beginning to decline.[3] Short-termism attitudes in the younger generations, the fact that we are facing what Ravi Zacharias calls "the feelings generation" is not helping us grow in wisdom. It's stifling it. As mentioned before, the stats for teenage pregnancy are the lowest they've been in many, many years, but STDs are on a substantial rise. We're not making wiser decisions, we're making decisions that please ourselves, avoiding responsibility, empathy, and foresight, actions that are never based on consequences or long-term goals.

So how do we acquire this noble wisdom that sets our Christianity apart from other faiths? That sets us apart from those who consider themselves postmodern and in keeping with today's moral culture? We pray. We remind ourselves that we do not always know what is best for us. We consciously choose ways to build trust with ourselves, our instinct, our hearts. We pray for the gift of discernment. We pray that we might notice the details in others. We surround ourselves with like-minded believers, while seeking ways to love those yet to believe.

True kingdom wisdom has distinctive values that, compared to other options, are delectable to the spiritual taste buds.

Wisdom researches beyond what feelings tell us. Apathy waits for life to teach us a lesson.

Wisdom welcomes rebuke, inviting the short leash of correction in search of excellence. Ignorance makes do with the circumstance, never looking beyond our own needs and desires.

Wisdom learns from unlikely sources, gathering experts

from across the world. Idiocy searches for no one, doing the same thing over and over again, expecting a different outcome.

Wisdom is observant, asking questions before allowing personal hurts to take shape. Asininity hears half a story and concludes the rest of the tale from previous experience.

Wisdom does not reside in intelligence alone, but has the humility to always ask the heart of the Lord on a matter. The prideful miss out by assuming education buffers every other opinion.

Wisdom plans its response. The thoughtless react instantly.

Wisdom seeks no argument. The antagonistic want nothing more.

The wise win souls. The inept perform for approval, losing souls entirely.

Wisdom never excuses but persists. The insolent persist in their excuses.

The wise find ways to be compassionate. Fools find ways to exert their opinions.

Wisdom never exceeds intimacy without trust. The inept give their heart and soul to a stranger.

The wise bear fruit with stories that travel a thousand years. The bewildered only hope that this could have been their story.

This gift is of wisdom not necessarily found in the most successful leader of the company, or in Ivy Leaguers with the finest education. It can come to a young boy at twenty quicker than an ego-ridden eighty-year-old minister who once had an anointing somewhere during the sixties crusades. The only difference is one realized he could never have wisdom without the guidance of the Lord. The other lived on the fumes of testimonies from four decades ago.

Wisdom cannot be accessed with goodwill or by reading a thousand books.

It can only be found in the gated acres of heaven, and the only One who holds the keys is willing to give them to you.

If only we would ask.

FOR SELF-REFLECTION

There is a difference between the educated elite and divine wisdom. Daniel is a beautiful example of how to carry out godly wisdom. True wisdom seeks understanding and is marinated in meekness.

It never assumes; it always inquires.

It is tough-minded and stable in storms of the turns of change.

It is often original and creative, sometimes opposing current law, but always scriptural.

It listens to a trusted committee and adheres to its advice.

There is a connection between purity and wisdom, truth and humility. In our honesty, the Lord will always guide us.

What are we doing wrong to not let the sinner believe we are approachable? In what ways could we all be more compassionate?

True wisdom does not divide but brings peace.

FROM WISDOM TO FACING PAIN

Most hurt is caused by unmet pain. If we do not confront that which we do not want to with wisdom, with courage, with trust in Him, we are no friend to ourselves, never mind to others.

"He was one of those, who was there for you at 3:00 a.m., when I could taste gun metal on my lips."
—MICHAEL BRAVERMAN

CHAPTER 9

SUNT LACRIMAE RERUM

FACING PAIN

She was nineteen, single, and pregnant. Although her mother was with her, she sat opposite me, shaking.

A decade ago I was a pregnancy crisis counselor. I volunteered on my days off from the advertising world. I was also still journeying through my questions of faith, through agnostic ambivalence, and I was so perturbed by the extreme ways fundamentalists had treated girls left in this kind of bind, I was, at this time, pro-choice. Little did I know that meeting these women would actually change my own convictions. Ironically, these values had nothing to do with my return to faith, but more with what this whole saga was doing to girls, both born and unborn. This was the year I would learn more than ever about how poorly we process pain, how too often we live in denial, fixing a mess with a scripture or some quick-witted solution. How rarely we embrace the *sunt lacrimae rerum*—"The tears of things."

"I don't want to keep it," she told me firmly, looking at her mother for a response. Her mother nodded.

"Are there any particular reasons why?" I whispered.

"I'm single. I've no money. I struggle enough as it is. The father doesn't want to know. He didn't even wanna wear protection."

"Sounds like a keeper," I retorted.

"My friends will not wanna hang out with me if I'm a mum. I can't do uni. I have nothing to offer the kid. Need me to go on?"

It was a typical story, a pattern of fear and adamant control of what they can still feel powerful in—a pattern I often saw play out in that very chair in my office. She was looking at her mother more than anyone else in the room. Of course, the mothers are a great comfort during these moments, but after asking a few questions, something wasn't adding up.

I asked the mother if it would be all right for her daughter and me to talk privately for a few minutes.

I had a template sheet that the center counselors used. We called it the head to heart diagram. A chart that asked what was the head saying and what was the heart saying. And if there are disconnections between the two. After caring for many women who had suffered post-abortion trauma, we took their advice and sought to help the women before a potential abortion. In this case, her head said to get rid of it, her head said she wouldn't cope, her head said the world believed it a bad idea. Her heart didn't have much to say. Other than it wouldn't be an easy week.

"Something isn't working for me though." I put my pen and paper on the table, next to the cup she had just peed in. The teller-of-truth cup, I liked to call it.

"Oh?" she said.

"Forgive me for prying, but we are here to help you find a path that looks at all angles. You're telling me you don't want this baby, and I can completely understand all the reasons you gave me as to why you wouldn't want to go through this entire life-changing thing. But why would a girl who doesn't want to keep it stop drinking and smoking while she's pregnant?"

There was a little silence. A little heaviness in the room. She was a ten-a-day smoker and loved to party. If you were wanting to be truly rid of any form of life, you wouldn't stop the party habits or the cigs. As with the ones who did truly want nothing to do with motherhood, they were sabotaging their pregnancy by every reckless lifestyle choice possible at this point.

"Between you and me and these walls, if I told you we have the resources, the money, even new parents, if necessary, to take care of this whole thing without an abortion, would your head be saying something different? Would your heart have a little more airtime?"

"I'm too young to have my own say. My family is scared they'll have to take care of it. But honestly? I wondered why I was giving up the cigarettes and the booze."

I smiled, because, like the Samaritan woman, she was being honest for the first time. It might have been my closest to feeling what Christ did in the same moment. She smiled too.

"I think I'd really like to. And I know the dad doesn't wanna know. I was stupid to not think about this before. But my dad isn't around, and I did alright? Apart from right now . . ."

I reinforced that it was her decision, not anybody else's, but we try to look at what people are doing, not what they are saying. For the heart can be the most silenced voice in the process, yet it's that part that causes the most pain if it goes unanswered. It's the functioning part that Christ tries to get to with us the most, but the majority of us ignore its existence.

She asked her mother back in and found the courage to tell her that she wanted to keep it. The mother found the courage to tell the daughter that secretly she was hoping for a little grand-child, but she didn't want her daughter to feel the pressure. And after entering into the office with fear and trepidation, she left triumphant, nervous, but truthful to what her heart really wanted. As a spectator, I had to watch these stories week in and week out.

We'd get phone calls from the hospital with girls screaming in horror, asking why no one had told them the abortion would be like this. Why hadn't they been told that they'd see what was coming out, this tiny fetus that could fit in the cup of their hands—that it was this graphic?

"Because the government doesn't want to upset any teen-ager who might have already gone through what you are going through. We are not allowed to tell you the truth of what goes on in a school setting. They're frightened of the girls facing shame," I said disappointedly on the phone.

"So instead they send us into the fire unprepared? If they told us the truth, maybe fewer of us would be in this mess. I don't know how I'll ever erase this from my mind." She sobbed, sinking down the wall of the bathroom in a hospital gown. In only a few minutes she went from the potential of motherhood to a single, mourning girl.

I had no words, no comfort for her. Other than a desire to see if we could start getting the schools to talk about identity, honor, love, and perhaps later about how to process pain—something I believe is vital for every home, never mind every educational curriculum.

My mother was a hospital chaplain, and far too many times women would call the hospital asking what they had done with the fetus from her abortion five years before, asking if my mum, by any chance, had said a blessing over it. Mum decided to do just that, because she knew this pain would rupture into the atmosphere for most women who had made this choice in a dark time.

This isn't a pro-life chapter, nor part of some agenda against Planned Parenthood; we have no time for that. There are greater things at stake—the individuals of the modern era for starters. No. This is a story to demonstrate that God wired our hearts toward life, toward joy, and toward enlightenment. And when we face anything that is the opposite to that, the heart mourns. Pain is stubborn, resilient. It stays in the foundations of the soul until it's been given its time in front of the jury to present its case. So rarely does pain get such a luxury. Instead, it comes back to haunt us in our dreams, in our most intimate relationships, in our trust, in our confidence, in our perspective on people. Forgiveness is uttered in prayer, in a whimsical statement across a living room, but the bitterness keeps showing up in triggering moments because the person hasn't actually processed pain. There cannot be a shortcut. There is no way around pain.

It's what the crisis center was made for, to counsel, to help women grieve because what they believed was just a standard procedure actually had feelings and emotions attached. Despite what the pro-choice campaigners tell you. For every one protester, there were ten women in our office distraught. The panic of responsibility, the fear of failing their parents was enough to suffocate their own broken hearts.

There's something about processing pain that we mustn't ignore. To ignore pain would be to deny your true self. To deny that it is a gift. The curse of leprosy is that it eats at the nervous system so that you no longer feel pain; and with pain numbed, injuries and deformities develop. It's no different when it comes to the soul. And if we are in denial, we will be in denial within our greatest relationship—with God. Denial hinders the full freedom we could obtain. This is where the noble become the ignoble; where the potentially good people cause havoc in their relationships; where the world leaders break up their families, confessing their sexual misdemeanors on national television; where the headmasters find themselves in prison; why the evangelist tries to sooth his pain at the bottom of vodka bottles; why workplaces are filled with infidelity.

We've all been too chicken to cross the proverbial pain road.

Today, headlines like "Badly behaved pupils driving teachers out of profession" paint the press. "Books related to finding happiness climbed 83 percent from a year ago." Anxiety is increasing, with 300 million people on the planet suffering from anxiety-related issues,[1] while 25 percent of Britain has a drinking problem. More kids at age eleven are clicking on porn than clicking on Amazon, and 40 percent more wives are having affairs than in 1990.[2]

I don't believe the stats would be this startling if we knew how to process pain. If we targeted the real issues rather than turning to pain killers that suffocate the real issues.

The concept of processing pain may seem a little out of sync with the preceding chapters. It's the negative pointer. It's the uninspiring token of the book. But we're in act three now, the crescendo of *The Noble Renaissance*. And to put it bluntly, this is where the noble can slip up. Pain creates either dysfunction or internal power. Never both. And by now, the chapters might be building to a point of exhaustion. Filling you with fear, that any tiny slip, any undercharged packet of chewing gum that goes amiss represents our callus lack of heart. I don't wish you to give up because the stakes seem so high; I wish you to be inspired. Full of compassion toward yourself. Although the noble may have hearts for excellence, there is no excuse for perfectionism, for the latter is full of self-hatred, a never-ending carousel of displeasure.

Being honest with ourselves, being brave when facing pain saves a lot of heartbreak for many around us.

Even if we ignore the pain, it will not ignore us.

And that's the false pretense that the world often lives with. That time will heal, that keeping busy will distract, that pushing forward will soothe the trauma. But if that were the case, why are there so many people unable to cope? Seeking solace in kundalini or Bikram yoga won't build character or challenge you in the most intense moments.

Cocaine, porn, affairs, codependency, agoraphobia are culprits of this uneducated psychosis, while Vicodin is financially endorsed by our unmet pain. Our unmet sense of powerlessness.

C. S. Lewis put it best: "We can ignore even pleasure. But pain insists upon being attended to. God whispers to us in our pleasures, speaks in our conscience, but shouts in our pain: it is his megaphone to rouse a deaf world."[3]

How many of you read my references to Martin Luther King Jr. and questioned if he should be on the noble list? What about the forty women he allegedly had affairs with? How many of you read the recent articles on Gandhi and refuted my choice of placing him in this book? There, I said it. The elephant is not just acknowledged in the room; it's ruined all the furniture. I have a friend who met Martin Luther King Jr., worked with him, and although he loved the work he witnessed from his courage, bravery, and brilliant method in nonviolence, my friend reminded me of the liberal nature he walked in. I suggested that Martin Luther King Jr. lived in a time when pain and torment had no outlet, no space to truly process apart from the prayer closet. When did he have the time for such, when much of his time was behind closed bars? Perhaps, in my novice analysis, he had some pain—the physical destruction of his home, the humiliation of prejudice, the heartache of inequality—and that in itself was enough for him to need comfort, a sexual numbing from the trappings of the world watching him. I don't condone, but like our Lord, I try to understand.

For Gandhi, only the Lord and only witnesses present know what truly took place in his household, and the Lord knows how my heart for the truth never wishes to defend anything not of Him. Yet I wonder just how much harder it becomes for those placed on the pedestal to be fully honest with themselves now, never mind anyone else.

Whether it's justification or full-blown denial, we are a lot further away from fighting a noble fight if we can't clean up our messes, if we don't have the courage to face our own inner turmoil.

It's a fine reminder that even the most famously noble are still human. Nobility is not seeking perfection; it's seeking growth and God's heart on all matters.

In our lack of processing, we cause pain in others—often the ones closest to us.

My own sweet father struggled with the idea of counseling, docking it in the station of selfish introspection. Because he refused to look at earlier situations in his life, I suffered some of the side effects. Some of his heartache. He's no longer around, for what I believe to be this reason alone; the unwillingness to look at pain.

I mean, it's not exactly fun. Dad preferred to dance around the living room with me or play practical jokes. He wished to align with the kingdom perspective of joy. But if we are truly powerful in God's sight, if we can take on all aspects of earth, then we can face directly, much like our Lord in the garden of Gethsemane, the anguish of earthly battles.

During my own mourning of my father, I discovered I couldn't process pain. Crying was the only process I knew, but

I was stagnant in moving forward. It would take me six years of busyness, codependency, a twenty-a-day smoking habit, an arrogance of opinions and bitterness, flighty career paths, and incessant perfectionism to make me realize I was as terrible at handling pain as Pops was.

The heart refuses to budge, stubborn in its need to be heard. The failure of today's culture is that it needs to be heard by the one who caused it pain, but the truth is, the Lord is the definitive therapist; He gets to speak into this as long as we are honest. No official apology, no heartfelt sentiment from the culprit can help you build your character. Sometimes I wonder if in their lack of awareness, their lack of remorse, we truly get to test our hearts' nature. We see whether we will resort to victimhood, stuff everything down with more performance, or write a different ending in our minds so we don't have to face the humanity of it all.

In my own dilemmas as a pastor, I realized I needed to make room for my younger students, to understand the same need for pain and its process.

"Meet me at 3:00 p.m. at this address," I said as I slipped a note to one of my students.

"Are we not meeting in your office? Like we usually do?"

"Not today. All will be revealed later on." I winked and left her curious. She kept wondering if she had done something wrong, if this was the address where I "removed" students from the church to my underground lair for the difficult cases, where they may never be seen again.

Apprehensively, she turned up to the address, just a usual house on a usual street with the front door slightly ajar. As she pushed the door open, she found a huge stand-alone punching bag. Next to it was me, sitting on the floor, holding a pair of boxing gloves.

"Time to let it out, my love."

She smiled, terrified, unsure what to make of all this, but delighted that someone would want to take the time for her soul—and equally petrified of what might come out. She'd been pent up for decades. And in some ways, it had worked for her. Years of hurt, isolation, anger, disappointment, abandonments, self-hatred, bitterness—these emotions focused on those who raised her were all ready to have a conversation. Even if she didn't want to.

Facing pain is a masterful, magical art. Only the bravest can attest to the gift of it, while the rest hide behind their distractions, their codependency, their pathetic control. "To live is an awfully big adventure," as J. M. Barrie wrote in *Peter Pan*, but so few truly live life to the fullest as they numb themselves to the earthly pain that we must all face.

"I'm going to be in this with you the whole time," I said.

"That's what I'm worried about," she whispered. "Why would anyone love me after what they are about to see?"

"Well, this is the beauty of it. If I don't think you're reaching to the levels of true expression, I'm going to encourage you. But otherwise, just get going. See where the Holy Spirit wants you to start."

She inhaled with the readiness to start running at the bag, but she false started, and said, "What if I cuss in front of my pastor?"

This wasn't about condoning a potty mouth, but about disallowing these polished performances we so often give to the Lord in prayer. I gave her the room to lose it, to get mad, to finally expel all the bitterness; I gave her the gloves too—but she didn't know what to do, frightened of her most free self. She was experiencing what any human with a heart experiences—the fear of unleashing it all. *What if I open the floodgates and the tears never stop? Is this not an invite for the men in white coats to disguise the trip to the asylum as a "fun day out"? What if I discover some truth that I'm not ready for? What if God rejects me after He sees how dark my heart really is?* We say what we hope He might want to hear, but, oh, how such attempts insult Him. For He didn't just see it all; He has been waiting for this moment, for us to clear the air with ourselves so that He may come in closer.

"What if you don't do anything, and you stay stuck in anger for the rest of your days? I need you to think of the effect this has had on your relationships, on your own heart. It is time." I held her shoulder for a minute. There's something about human contact that I swear our Lord was so good at.

She took a deep breath, closed her eyes in the hope she'd open them and find herself in a meadow—without me there. But between the Lord, the punching bag, and me, she wasn't going anywhere. Too many of us wanted her free from her own limited thinking.

Beginning quietly, she whispered the memories that hurt her, moments she was left to fend for herself. The volume increased as she saw that I wasn't leaving, she heard me in the background, sounding excited that she was being honest. She began to get louder, finding her voice in the pain. The anger increased; she soon forgot I was in the room, and *really*, and I mean *really*, began to punch it out. Her entire ordeal lasted for just fifteen minutes. And in a final punch, she fell to the floor in tears, as I walked over and held onto her. Letting her cry. I won't deny it—I cried too. The trauma she had gone through was enough to make Quentin Tarantino blush.

Many might process pain to this point; we might have a good ol' cry and think we are healed. We leave the confessional box. We expose our flawed ways to another human and heave a sigh of relief.

"I feel much better, thank you."

"Oh, we're not done." I smiled.

"What?" She didn't smile.

"You can't excavate a wound and leave it open; you have to fill it with the good stuff."

And this is where Holy Spirit whispers to the open heart, sweet somethings that don't just flatter or fill the void but change perspectives, filling us with compassion to bring us wisdom and an overwhelming sense to forgive because we finally gave a voice to our hearts. And we change. We become different. No longer do we look to another to resolve this pain; nor do we add their faults to the back catalogue we have been holding accounts with.

People know how to cry, how to vent anger, but they haven't been taught how to ask questions after their speech is concluded. It's here where insight is vital, where we find understanding of ourselves. We ask questions like: How has this whole event affected other people around me? How did this leave me? Are my current attitudes working for the greater good of others? What do I do now that I've processed this honestly with you?

Is this biblical, you ask? Does this have any resonance for the holy of holies?

Let's take a closer look at the garden of Gethsemane.

Christ invited Peter and a couple of disciples to join Him as He prayed. The disciples did what we would likely have done at the late hour—slept. But Christ had advised them to "pray that you may not enter into temptation" (Matthew 26:41 ESV).

Pain in prayer is not just a matter of finding forgiveness; it looks ahead of time. His wisdom always took the futuristic path, and like cleaning your teeth with the hygienist, He took the preventive measures. Perhaps He just wanted company in His most terrifying hour; perhaps He was modeling the rawest way to pray for the friends who needed it the most. Regardless of His motives, it's the story I come back to again and again. The tearing of the clothes for King David was the sweating of the blood for our Lord. There's a bargaining. A plea. Like any true relationship that involves sacrifice, it invokes an honest dialogue that trusts the listener to consider all odds. It's guttural. Expressive. Pure. It surrenders while acknowledging the humanity of our own limitations. And as the angel came to comfort Jesus, He despaired more. Knowing that there could be no other option than to be crucified, to feel the metal piercing His hands. To suffocate in front of mockers and a doting mother. The most perilous pain to date. How ironic that we cry out to our Lord, wondering why we have to face such pain ourselves, thinking that His dying for our sins meant we would be delivered of pain completely.

This is part of living on earth. The quandary of pain and plight, joy and euphoria, the good versus evil. But as life resurrected three days later, so, too, does the pain of our sorrow lift. And with the honesty of pain comes the exuberance of joy. You cannot have one without the other.

It was in reading the witness of Christ's pain after John the Baptist's death, His weeping over Lazarus' death, and the disturbing dialogue in the garden of Gethsemane that I learned how often pain is the introduction to joy. To numb it is to never experience the fullness of joy. If we never relate to pain, we never find compassion, the main expression that pulls out the red carpet for a miracle.

Does this mean we walk around looking for pain and depression? Does this mean we dine with introspection or have supper with melancholy? No. For the true process of pain is a dialogue with God, not a monologue with ourselves. That's when you know you are processing pain correctly.

You are conversing with a kind Father. A warm person who

is always on your noblest side. It may bring you news that makes you sweat blood, but the result could be that it saves the world from the grips of hell.

The noble, in all they face, in the drudgery of this world, never fear pain, nor react to people based on previous pain, because, unlike many, they've already found the compassion of a kind Father before the deed was ever done. Paul had conquered this only too well: "I now rejoice in my sufferings for you, and fill up in my flesh what is lacking in the afflictions of Christ, for the sake of His body, which is the church" (Colossians 1:24).

Just as Jesus dipped the bread into the wine and gave it to Judas the night of His arrest, so, too, did He choose to suffer for the sake of us all.

How can we choose to suffer for our Lord if we're frightened to suffer the tears of things?

FOR SELF-REFLECTION

Pain is a gift and must be acknowledged through all walks of life. Numbing pain disinvites His wisdom into the problem, never allowing us to find resolution. Pain is rarely fixed by another; even the brilliant therapists out there cannot build you in the way that the Lord can.

Through honesty in pain comes exquisite and divine wisdom.

If you do not believe God is good or kind, find ways to resolve that lie. For until you can trust Him with it all, you will live in denial. Denial is the killer of all healing processes.

Processing pain correctly should not need to take years or hurt others along the way.

Pray always with honesty so that you may resist temptation.

Be vulnerable with others; isolation is another form of avoiding pain.

How will we know He can be our strength if we never give Him our weakness?

FROM FACING PAIN TO LOVE

The freedom to be noble lies in
the belief of whether or not you
belong in the throne room.

CHAPTER 10

ANGELS OF MERCY

LOVE

He carried a crowbar in his back pocket. Albeit vertically challenged (I'm trying to be polite here), he packed a mighty punch in fights. Very few ever contested or dared face the challenge of overcoming Wrex. He was your quintessential British mod, aggressively proud of it and his Piaggio Vespa, although not so proud of his broken family. It was 1969, and a local Baptist minister, Tony, was walking to a service one evening when Wrex and his gang began following Tony up the street. The minister began to run as Wrex hurled expletives, mocking him for owning a biker's club when he was a Baptist minister. There was no point trying to reason, or even standing to fight, and he was walking very close to the entrance of the 171 Club, a Hells Angels club based in Manchester, England.

Now, this is a true story, so you need not suspend your belief for these next few paragraphs.

As Tony eyed the club, Wrex was getting closer; then Tony began to suffer an asthma attack. He managed to run down the stairs to the 171 Club and flee behind the curtain. Wrex followed down the steps, crowbar in hand, pulling back the red velvet drape to find a sea of black leather—three hundred bikers to be exact. The noise from the jukebox had stopped, as had the chatter. Cigarette smoke was clearing, and as Tony tried to gain any ounce of oxygen, the bikers saw the alien nonresident threat on the steps to the club. You wear a suit like that, holding a weapon, you're likely to be a mod with a treacherous agenda. This was the sixties, the era not just of the Mary Quant jersey dress and free-loving Woodstock, but the rivalry between the mods and the rockers. The suits and the leathers. The scooters and the Ducatis. The Rolling Stones hired one team of Hells Angels to be their security team for their gigs, knowing such a presence would keep everything in order. Until one of the Hells Angels stabbed someone. Then things just got ugly from there. The communities despised the rise of the Hells Angels clubs, but Tony, a Baptist minister in his late twenties, was trying to save these boys from their own name.

Wrex had no clue what he had just gotten into, but it wasn't looking good.

The bikers were very protective of "the Rev" because it was Tony who had guided these same bikers away from the brink of jail, addiction, violence, and squalor. It began after Tony answered a call from some local neighbors complaining of the chaos seven boys were causing on the Abbey Hey Estate, one of the poorest communities in Manchester. Tony turned up on his motorbike. The Rev said the boys were "just bored" and built them a room in the underground cellar of an abandoned church hall. The boys were only seventeen when the club began. Tony took the seven of them under his wing, knowing most had no fathers, no jobs, no sense of purpose. From there the club grew, with a film room, a game room, the great hall, and a sweet shop that needed cats to chase out the rats. It was dark, filled with feathered hairstyles, and the coolest thing going in Manchester. Now there were hundreds of people there, and not all were necessarily bikers, but men from all classes, all industries, wearing their 171 Club badge with pride, even if they took the number 52 bus to get there. So when the bikers saw the Rev scrambling in his pockets for an asthma spray, one of the bikers shouted:

"GERRRRRUUUUMMMM!!!!"

The bikers charged, like the scene from *Braveheart* without Mel Gibson's eloquent motivational speech, and within a second Wrex was being chased by three hundred rockers.

The Rev, seeing the tidal wave of leather flood his way, followed Wrex up the stairs again. He watched Wrex jump over a wall opposite the entrance to hide, and as the rest of the gang dispersed, the bikers wanted to know which way Wrex had gone. Tony pointed in the opposite direction to throw off the fight. The bikers ran down the street.

Once the coast was clear, Tony looked over the wall to see a huge drop, with Wrex at the bottom, writhing in silent pain. He had broken his ankle.

Tony looked to his wife, May, who was just catching up with what had happened from the kitchen: "You up for taking a trip to the hospital?" May and Tony loaded Wrex onto the back of her bike, and St. Mary's hospital gained a new patient that evening. Wrex was moved that they were willing to help at all, considering he was about to tear the Rev apart with a metal instrument. Kindness always leads to repentance, but so often people like Wrex refuse to accept kindness at all, unless immobile. Only the noble, only those who know true sonship, offer kindness when we're threatened.

The incident from crowbar to the infirmary had reminded Tony of how far the boys had come. (Charging angrily toward an aggressive gang of mods aside.) Because the bikers used to be like Wrex. They were robust, stubborn. Ready for a fight at any notice. Prouder of their weapons than of their backgrounds. The absence of a father left them entitled to take everyone else's happiness. In their fathers' rejection, they attempted to find refuge in pillaging, unethical power, punches, and a pack mentality. For them, everything had to be equal, everything had to be fair. No one could be celebrated in promotion or favor if the same wasn't being dealt to each one. They were cloaked in comparison, competition, and cowardice—guised as beating each other to a pulp. This wasn't exclusive to broke boys in Manchester; this is becoming the situation in today's generation, the most fatherless generation to date.

Like the biker boys, people are on a constant search for who is going to be loyal, who has longevity in the trust game. There is no room for human error, no room for love. To request a smile from these biker boys turned out to be as effective as getting a toddler to read *Hamlet*. For there was nothing to smile about. But when Tony came into their lives, the scripture that kept echoing in his mind was 1 John 4:19: "We love because He loved us first" (NIV). Tony also had a difficult upbringing. His father was present but emotionally absent, and the only thing that changed the course of his story was the love of a heavenly Father that he encountered at twenty-one. A love that softened him, turning his gaze outward to the needs of others. That's what true sons do. They serve not *for* love, but *from* it.

Tony knew that even if the bikers had found Wrex, they'd have confronted his motives, asked for the crowbar, and told Wrex to get a new hobby, perhaps even choose a new kind of transport. But they wouldn't have fought back anymore. They'd have invited him in. That's the change, the difference in being loved.

Things were different now they belonged.

Everyone is always different when we belong. When we are seen, unquestionably loved, fought for, covered, protected, guided, observed, gently confronted, understood, secure, believed in, educated, invested in, devoted to, inspired, forgiven seventy times seven, shown compassion, doted on, adored, explained to, abundantly blessed by, sacrificed for, present in, listened to, counseled by, and qualified by nothing other than the beautiful fact that we exist. Such tenderness overrides the need to protect ourselves.

At last, there is a rest in our souls.

It is this that motivates, that decides our response. And when we have no father or mother, when we are so quickly exposed to a life absent of any quality of love, we have no choice other than to survive. At least that's what we were once taught. It's what many Christians still struggle in accepting—that in love's presence we live like kings. In love's absence, we die inwardly—morally, spiritually, fundamentally—in all sectors of life.

It is being loved that beckons us to nobility. I'm not certain we can make noble sacrifices without it. Without a sense of love, we have no desire to sow love. In the most fatherless generation to date, this is why we as a world are struggling. Why prejudice overrides kindness, why political opinions are bulldozing peace and puffing up the chests of the ignorant.

It's well known, through psychology and sociology reports, that children raised without the presence of a father will more often than not show more signs of immoral and delinquent behavior than those raised with a father.

One report states:

The more opportunities a child has to interact with his or her biological father, the less likely he or she is to commit a crime or have contact with the juvenile justice system (Coley and

Medeiros, 2007). In a study of female inmates, more than half came from a father-absent home (Snell, Tracy, & Morton, 1991). Youths who never had a father living with them have the highest incarceration rates (Hill, O'Neill, 1993), while youths in father-only households display no difference in the rate of incarceration from that of children coming from two-parent households (Harper and McLanahan, 2004).[1]

Although we entered into a Christian commitment with our Lord, with the finest Father one could ever wish for, we still act like orphans. As if we never engaged with this furious love of our Father. As if we were released from the shackles but we are still sitting in prison, with the door unlocked and wide open. The true reason Christ acted with such nobility was that He was rooted, established, and believed in by a tender Father who governs the mightiest kingdom for all. He was a true heir, a son and Son of God, a walking testament to tell us we could be the same. That we could come home now. Fully embraced by His heart. That we, too, could be heirs to a glory that could topple the kings of darkness. This is teaching that only a few Pharisees truly grasped. A teaching that is often lost on the fearful Christian standing in front of a demoniac.

It was fatherlessness that gripped one friend into the darkness of the Church of Satan. Night after night he found his identity in darkness, in the occult, in spiritual warfare. He was ranked as a Night General. Astral-projecting hatred, depression, lust over areas of New York City. For years he took joy in the pain of others, paid thousands to curse the innocent. But too often he noticed that when he tried his works on Christians, he couldn't penetrate the authority they carried. His spells didn't work. He was tired, exhausted from his years on night shift, and in his request for a sabbatical, Satan made him blind. Physically blind for one year. This is when he began to question the true heart of Satan. For a long time, he'd been told something different. And in an encounter one night, Jesus found my friend in his dreams. So close was Satan to killing him for his betrayal, the fatherly touch of the shining God brought him back home. For the first time in decades, the gangster from New York City had felt Christ's tenderness. And because of that, He began fighting for the freedom of others. Teaching the power that Christians have in God, to not misunderstand what their Father is doing for them.

And today so many of God's followers make agreements, come into union with prideful, vengeful, accusatory quests for their own lives to be redeemed by the demise of another. We are ignoble because we have not truly believed with the fullness of our hearts that we can be fully loved in our mess. That there is enough love to go around for everyone. That we are deserving of a love so zealous and hungry for our gaze; despite what we have done, such love runs us at a fever pitch.

So why are so many Christians lukewarm?

This orphan thinking is evident in delinquents living in Rikers prison, New York's most intense penitentiary, or in the suits of Wall Street. It is not affected by the scenery. My friend Pastor Rex has ministered to men in prison, most serving life, teaching them about the goodness of God, the love of His heart for them. The length of time it takes for them to begin to believe in this "good God" depends on the openness of their hearts, their willingness to listen. For some it takes years; for others it takes a day, because they know their ways, their hopeless beliefs haven't been serving them well. Pastor Rex has grown to love these men like his own sons, and he has served them for long enough to see them set free, not just from the gray walls of Rikers, but most importantly from themselves. They are finally able to nurture and guide their own families. But it came with a great sacrifice, which meant Pastor Rex had to first encounter God's love. His father had introduced him to cocaine by the time he was twelve. He began to deal drugs himself on the borders of Colombia by the time he was sixteen. Whether they're villains or the good cops, we always want to please our daddies. The problem for Pastor Rex was that he was trying to please the villain. And it was a heavenly Father who took over and introduced Rex to a new way of living. One that loved, that didn't steal due to lack but shared due to a faith in an abundant Father. He went from pauper to prince within a week. And from there, nobility was just a matter of refining week by week, year by year.

It doesn't concern the son or daughter how their life began. Even if your head has experienced the heavy weight of the coronation crown, you could still be an orphan thinker. Even if a boy lives on the streets of Calcutta, washing himself in the gutters, he could still think and act like a prince, depending on how he views himself. The silver platters or the squat buckets are inconsequential; it's the internal struggle that echoes the scripture, "For as he thinks in his heart, so is he" (Proverbs 23:7).

On the wall in my study is a quote: "Who we are is determined by the amount we have allowed Him into our hearts."

How we receive honor is indicative of whether we think like an heir to a kingdom God created for us to play in or whether we don't believe we deserve anything.

After three years of ministry school at Bethel Church, I was invited to apply for a role as a pastor at their school. It's a job that at least one hundred people apply for each year, and there were only two spots available. For others this was a door to a whole new life, one filled with revival, transforming individuals, and watching the Lord break people to reveal their true selves. But for me, although I loved the leaders, and admired all their work, I wanted to run faster than Tony had that night to the 171 Club.

As the time came closer for an interview, I had to make a decision. I called on everyone for advice. I heard nothing distinctly from the Lord, and yet I heard clearly from everyone around me: What was my alternative?

"You remind me of my daughter," my pastor told me. "I've never seen as much favor on anyone as I have on you within this church, more than I've had, and I've been working here for ten years. But you're not aware of it. When I want to come and play with my daughter, she is too busy on the iPad for me. But when she wants to play, I'm already at work. There's an invite that you're not taking, and I wonder why."

I drove home asking the same question. And on the dark roads of California, as my headlights lit up the pines, I finally heard God.

My little lady.

I always know it's Him, for His voice is soft, enticing, deep, and reverent. Much like Mufasa from *The Lion King*. His voice is home for me; His tenderness breaks me into tears every time, like the school calling your mum to come pick you up and that sense of relief when you see your mother's face. That everything will be all right.

"Papa?"

You have served Me and My heart for a long time now. But you've never stretched and served at the same time. It is time, little one, to stretch your capacity and to find Me at the end of it.

The words put more fear into me than I can describe.

But, of course, He was right. I had worked as a freelancer by this point. I could pick up and put down jobs. I could work according to my schedule, my fears. I never had to stretch beyond what was comfortable for me. And there was something about being employed by a team I had respected and admired for so long—they were coming too close.

The next day, I burst into Bill Johnson's office. It's always peaceful there.

"I can't do it. I can't take the job. I'm too scared."

Bill didn't flinch or try to explain the reasons I'd be good for the job. He probably asked the Lord first before asking me what was going on.

I interrupted the silence. "You see, Bill, you and I are good. You know? We hang. We laugh. We're on what the UN would call 'good peaceful terms.' I fear in my being employed by you all this will change. That I'll get it wrong."

He chuckled like he does.

"Oh, you'll get it wrong." He smiled.

I gasped even harder this time.

"What if you took the job. And learned what it would be like to be loved whenever you got it wrong?"

The concept was an anomaly, an unorthodox approach to theology, surely. "You mean to say, that as a pastor, if I get it wrong, you will still believe in me?"

In previous employment I had the occasional telephone thrown at my head and often heard someone yelling my name from a walkie-talkie. I had been verbally shot down and blown up, mocked and humiliated, discredited or fully blamed, depending on the outcome of my actions. To be loved in my imperfection, well, that hadn't been my experience so far. So why would it change now? Besides, church environments didn't always do much better. Emails were still filled with assumptions, put-downs, snide remarks, and manipulations. The heart was the same, just less blatant. Moral failures in the church were met with lawyers and disciplinary actions. Although one thing I did know, even in moral failure in my church: people still stayed family, even if responsibilities toward others had to be given time out for a season. And now, had everything turned on its head, focusing on what was better for the soul more than the salary? I know Christ was like this; I know He is unconditionally loving, but the rest of the world (and those are the ones I have to work with), according to my record, wasn't.

And so, in this alarming discovery, I had to make the decision—to be open enough to let love into my ugliest confessions. To my most failed failures. To my mistakes. They knew my flaws as a student, but now that I was family, the cost was higher.

Day by day, week by week, I was expected to love these students with unconditional love. A feat not easy to achieve it seems. But I tried with all my might. What I was receiving from my bosses and now evidently, my Lord, I must be willing to give the same. I must be the daughter of an all-loving Father, not the orphan of desolate abandonment. With no fatherly covering since I was twenty-three, I had some excuses ready up my sleeve.

As I went about my day, Bill would sometimes watch me. Someone would compliment my clothing for example, and I would brush it off, as I often did: "Oh, this old thing! I got it at some dodgy bargain bin basement sale."

I think over the year Bill had hoped I'd work this out myself, but I was not good at taking a compliment. Which was indicative of how I receive love in general.

After one particular "brush off," Bill subtly slapped my hand.

"I do that a lot, don't I?"

He smiled.

"Not that I'm counting, but that's the fourth time today."

You see, conviction is always a beautiful time to celebrate and, in that tender revelation, I was aware that sons and daughters know how to receive honor, without it puffing the ego. It is only from the ego that we refuse love. From a childlike heart, we embrace all that is given so we can share it consistently.

And it's there, right there, where I discover being a child of God is not even a choice, or something you can will yourself into believing; it's an undoing of the hardened case we put on ourselves. From the heartbreaks of others, from the abandonment, from the brokenness no one can mend. The guarding of our hearts but we so poorly miscontextualized to guard ourselves from everyone else, also guarded ourselves from Him. We belittled God's goodness with the deflection of man. We question how anyone could love that hard, when no one else has. It's here we create a performance, a need to not just survive but to count. And here, when we forgot, where before our feet hit the earth, we were already counted by a heaven that knew our name, that designed our essence, how we would talk, where we would live, whom we would love, whom we could affect. And they entrusted us to love, despite the odds.

It was there where the Lord had to be given right of way into all parts of me. This place, where we all learn to love with a willingness to suffer for another without enquiring about the refund policy.

This is where we burn, we light up, beyond what we mere mortals are capable of alone. We have no need to look back, for there is so much to look forward to. And we become childlike again, but only with a maturity that refuses to take itself too seriously or to feel it must be on top of the game. It trusts that if we have the right heart posture and we ask for help, all will be well.

There is enough for each of us; there is enough for my broken heart—and twice over. If I let Him in, I'll soon believe it. And in our privilege as a son or daughter of our heavenly Father, we get to play again. We are no longer defined by ex-boyfriends, divorces, losses, bankruptcy, miscarriages, gossip, misunderstandings, insecure bullies, or fatherlessness.

God's children and heirs to the kingdom end up having the same virtues. Because they are the same people.

A few weeks ago I met with a friend whom I first met at Lambeth Palace when I was fourteen. Lord George Carey was the Archbishop of Canterbury in 1994, the head of the Church of England, and the advisor to the queen. He's a humble and articulate man. I reached out to him twenty-five years later to ask about his thoughts on nobility. We had lunch at the House of Lords, the second chamber of Parliament. Filled with lords, ladies, barons, and baronesses, the House of Lords holds the task of making and shaping laws and checking and challenging the government's position of current proposed bills. I was lunching with a man who knew, despite being a lord himself, how being a child of God is truly defined by whether we believe we were created in His image or not. After dessert he said, "There's a room that I'd like to take you to. I think it will help with your book."

After leading me through the corridors of marble statues, the libraries, the great halls, he opened a huge oak door. I walked into the thick presence of God. To my right were beautiful Renaissance paintings, each one larger than a Range Rover, each one displayed as if it was a Rubens or a Raphael. Underneath each painting was the name of a virtue. Courtesy, Generosity, Mercy, Religion, Hospitality—five virtues that covered the walls of what I then discovered was the queen's throne room. Because to my left, was her throne. A kaleidoscope of color, gold, and velvet. *Heavy is the head that wears the crown*, I thought. But what an honor, what a reverence I could feel in the room for her chosen duty to suffer, to lay down her life for her country.

This one thing is true: the greater your ability to sit on the throne, the more willing you are to suffer for others.

And in this room God confirmed to me, in a whisper, that these virtues, the ones that were highlighted around the room and based on the honor code of the knights' table, were the same virtues required of nobility, the same ones we can only fully function in if we are fully in union with our adoption as a child of God. To be merciful is to be a true son.

To be noble is to be an heir to the throne. And considering the invite has been given to us before recorded time, it's only a matter of saying yes, the vulnerability to shed our own self-protection from another's choices, and the daring boldness to step into a different way of looking at ourselves. What a revelation it was that for all my life I had been trying to make the world safe before I could be me, when actually, I just had to make myself safe—and in my identity in Him, I can trust my responses to an unpredictable planet.

———

By 1976, the bikers had developed a new identity, a sense of true worth, not by theft or by thwarting the police, but by working with them. The Rev had asked the Manchester police what such a large group of bikers, now totaling a thousand members, could do for their community. Despite the community's hostility, he still wanted to help them. The police told Tony that the biggest problem they had was transporting blood and drugs to and from Manchester and Liverpool hospitals. The ambulances just weren't fast enough. But bikes were.

And just like that, the Rev, the police, and the once upon a time tearaway boys developed a method to transport blood from Manchester to Liverpool hospitals while the police blocked off the roads. As orphans, they were stealing lives; as sons, they were saving them. The press got hold of the story and had a field day. "With Mercy on the Pillion" read one headline. "Minister Leads Ton-Up Lads on Rescue Missions." The focus on others, on the city, began to turn the boys to men. And the most violent of all the bikers, a boy who had lost his dad very early in life, ended up marrying a girl in the club, and together they fostered 120 kids in his lifetime.

And my favorite headline of them all? The true testament to men who became sons of an all-loving God:

"Angels of Mercy."

FOR SELF-REFLECTION

Orphan thinking works with spirits of rejection, inferiority, fear, poverty, and self-pity. It is one of the primary ways the Enemy attempts to shut down intercession in someone's life.

Author Jack Frost wrote, "The orphan spirit is not something you can cast out, because it has ungodly beliefs and/or attitudes of our flesh that has been developing over a lifetime. It has become part of our personality and character."[2]

No matter what you have been born into, we are all prone to orphan thinking.

But fatherlessness creates a more difficult struggle to believe in a good father at all. Who we are is determined by how much we allow Him into our hearts.

What areas in your life still show orphan thinking? Comparison?

True royalty will be aware of the choice to carry the heavy crown.

Royalty share the same emphasis on certain virtues: religion, courtesy, generosity, hospitality, mercy.

True sonship welcomes back to the world life-saving mercy.

CONCLUSION

It is found in your kneeling at injustice. It is witnessed in your compassionate exchanges amid prejudice. It is rarely photographed, but you don't care about that. Because your nobility is conveyed, projected on giant canvases in the heavens. You adopt the orphans, house the lost, and feed the hungry. You are catching more breaths, because now nobility is found in you.

Nobility can always be found in you.

The rest doesn't matter anymore, be it supporting the left or the right, manipulative data configurations that sway the persuadables by the gods of Silicon Valley. The very platforms that were created to connect us on the Internet are now being weaponized to divide and conquer. But none of this matters. For you have a tough mind yet a tender heart. An unshakable faith that does not bend, that has an ever-fixed mark outside of circumstance, disappointment, or betrayal.

You have awakened to Romans 6:6. You are the Colossians 3:10 and the 2 Corinthians 3:18. You are renewed, refreshed, and brand sparklingly new. If you don't realize He died for you to be dead to your old ways, then peace is at stake. Love is at stake.

What Christ died for is at stake.

You are noble toward *injustice*. You take on the hits, the brunt of pain. You stand for those who have no voice, yet you pick your fights wisely. You do not retreat into the shadows or stay silent. You speak with truth, a truth that is always laced with kindness. A truth that seeks to ask questions, to understand above your own idiosyncrasies.

In the drama, you refuse to partner with the macabre, for chaos never takes residence in your day. Only peace is found in the river of your life, even in a season of pain. Because you want to sleep at night. There is a sovereignty in your responses to injustice, a very peaceful antithesis to wrath that becomes the most violent weapon in the kingdom. Much like the towel, the bread, the wine that broke a thousand lies, the grace that brought us back home.

In the wars, the division, your head is held never so high that people can't talk to you, but never so low that gossip is acceptable. You cover the cruel and protect your heart in all matters. If the cruel continue to berate you, you still open your arms to them, with a self-respect that doesn't allow curses to cross your threshold. You know where to draw the line, even if it means taking the punches for the next generation. You are generous to the core, never weighing the amount you give by what's in your wallet or what another did, but more by what is in your heart, what is in His wallet.

You are noble in *perseverance*. You rally the troops and intercessors in the fine seasons as much as in the waning winters. You are remarkable in pain. Ever facing the hits with cries to the Lord, but never at the Lord. Even in the darkest hour, you never question His goodness. For you know Him well. The people around you have noted it. Like the friends of Job, they are stunned at your loyalty, when you had every reason to walk away from Him. But you knew that walking away would be the very death of you. That there is no greater love than His comfort, no greater high than His throne room, no greater euphoria in heaven when faced with the aridity of death. You are noble through it all.

In secret you release the pain and anger of humanity, you kick betrayal in the shins a hundred times, but always while holding His hand. For you are safer there, behind closed doors, than when on display to those you love. They don't need to feel the effects of your hurt. Yet you are courageous enough to be honest with people. You let them into the rawness of confusion. You seek the ones with greater faith and ask them to stand until you can stand again. It was in your vulnerability to reach out, in your accountability to check your own bitter behaviors, that you rose taller than ever before. It is within these seasons that you knew your character gained a promotion and a promise, that prosperity was to come.

You are noble in *integrity*. Every small matter means something to you. Every dialogue, every word on your tongue, must only confess life and love. Anything else is washed away to the deepest seas. Your integrity surpasses the value of oil. For truth to you is what sets us all free. You stand for veracity above all matters. Always understanding that whatever you pour into the world, into another, He will pour into you. You are aware that no matter what you do, no matter the sins you've committed, He will always love you. But your integrity refuses to settle for mediocre apathy, for just getting by. You carry out the axioms, not because you live in constant fear—nor are you molded by perfectionism. For all you really care for is your love for Him. And in that, like a man fully in love with his wife, infidelity is never an option. Disobedience isn't an option. You love Him too much for that.

And in this you are eager to see how, in your brave honesty, He will show up. Because your faith is so strong that you know He will show up.

You are noble in *humility*. Always centered in your voice being heard by Him, you don't need the entire world to hear it also. You show up every day; come rain, shine, or rejection, you show up. You are so kind to yourself, you never have to run from you. You keep running to Him and in that you run to yourself. Ever able to be confronted with your failings, your mishaps, but knowing your strength never rides on your successes. That's the beauty of you. Your identity is always centered on how much He loves you. You spot the homeless man on the corner of the street above the celebrity center stage. You are wise, because you humbled yourself. And in your humility, they feel safe with you. You are approachable enough to share their souls with. Therefore you have the gift of counsel. The gift of vulnerability that always invites more wisdom.

You are noble in *self-sacrifice*. You seek to suffer before anyone else does. But only for the right reasons, never for the label of martyrdom or heroism. You sacrifice for peace, for love, for your family, for the stranger. Because it's who you are. Your vision is for the long haul, for the legacy after you. You are highly favored because of how much you sacrifice. You are the most generous and, therefore, the most abundant in gift giving. You do not weigh how much someone should be worth sacrificing for. For it's all discussed and attributed in the secret place. You are not frightened or weakened by fear. For you can face the pain of sacrifice, because your Daddy taught you what's waiting on the other side. It's how the Holy Spirit comforts you. You have a clear ear to listen to Him as He directs you on what to sacrifice, how to sacrifice, always looking at what He is about to do. You give your time, capacity, energy, finances, heart, fears, focus—your all.

You are noble in *courage*. Your unique trust in Him provides the ability to run into the lions' den. To stand in the flames of the fire. To take a bullet to the head. To stand during trials, to testify against the wicked, to shovel timidity into the pit of hell. You are the bravest in the room. Therefore, the most powerful to speak. Others talk of your bravery, your strength, and when they ask for a crate of it from you, you point to the heavens and tell them heaven is waiting to give them courage, if only they would ask. You are a freedom fighter who is motivated by what grieves the Lord. You fight on His behalf, co-laboring yet always taking ownership for every step you take. Never blaming God if something goes wrong, always praising God if it goes right. You are mighty in prayer, contending incessantly to heal the sick, raise the dead, deliver people from demons, and cleanse the lepers. Leprosy, like everything else, has stigma you have no time for. Propaganda is an entity, like a demon, that you laugh in the face of. You take on the frontlines, the death lines, the hurdles of yourself. You never avoid, never dissociate, never partner with procrastination. Nor do you numb yourself with addictions, with worldly fabrications, for Christ's modeling is too close to your heart to deny yourself of the pleasures of His majesty.

You are noble in *wisdom*. With a consort of advisors you are safe in the keeping of counselors. You are asked more questions than you give opinions. You research a person's heart before you take account of their sins. You are full of compassion because you read everyone through Christ's eyes. You speak, act, and believe in His truth. Your wise discernment keeps you from lusting, from lies, from deluded comforts. You are built to seek always how to sow and reap on earth for the sake of the kingdom, so you are searching for ways to plant more. In your lack of people pleasing, you found more wisdom. You took on the steadfastness of the Word over the ever-changing tides of culture. You are a leader who, despite having fifty-three members in your metaphorical football team, coaches them in fifty-three different ways. You care for the individual, the one, and seek God's wisdom in every case before seeking the counsel of another. Yet, you never use God's name to get your way. You are always teachable, always open to those around you, even when they say things you don't want to hear. You follow their advice and take full ownership of such. This is how your wounds became your wisdom.

And all these virtues take place because you are a son, a daughter, a child of God. Your kindness is as perennial as the grass because you stay so close to your Father. You name yourself a child, not in fear of the responsibilities of adulthood but because you are now aware of just how much you were made in His image. The only faith in the world that introduced us to the father-child dynamic is the only one I see fully reaping the real fruit of love. It is in this identity that you thrive. As a mother, father, leader, pastor, engineer, teacher, prophet, servant, friend, you thrive most in His arms. His belief in you sustains you in the fiercest storms. It is here that you actually grew up more, that autonomy, faith, courage, courtesy, and wisdom were now easy to carry out because you belong. You are no longer codependent but interdependent with God and all His children. You are at peace with all.

You play often. You are the diamond in the rough ride of life—one that is ever polishing its edges, but always because you were refined by His hands. You are more in love today than ever before. For in reflecting all the scenarios, all the stories that you had to hand over in trust to the heavens with kindness, grace, and mercy, you had to hand it back; for sons and daughters of God don't control, manipulate, or find ways to rid people of free will. Like Simba looking into the waters in *The Lion King*, after so much running the Holy Spirit has made you look in the mirror to remind you of who you are. And every time you made a noble move that reflected your original design, you discovered a gem, a dust of gold scattered over a new story line. You are not frivolous or fearful or fractious in thinking. You are ever seeking to model your Father in every scenario; it's how you bring on revival. In witnessing your works, more are ready to come home to the Lord. Oh, how many souls are saved because of your childlike posture. And boy, do you have fun. Forever finding the joy in all.

It might be a frightful feat to look upon these words and think you're *expected* to be like this. After all, life is not that simple. It's not. It's complicated, devious, and full of trickery. But the nobles have figured out a way. Understanding that God would not record so many stories in the Bible to inspire us with nobility if these virtues were not already designed, embroidered, threaded into our beings.

You are already noble, for Christ's crucifixion tells us so.

And our God didn't place these virtues, these stories in the Scripture, to tease you, to deflate your morale. He would not play out these colorful characteristics if they were not available at your fingertips, if they were not already in your bloodstream. Why else do we cry when we see the lost welcomed home or the blind gain sight? We are poised with a design that lights up when we see His brilliance play out in stories. Because that's home for us all.

Don't disqualify who you are by what you've done or the choices you made—for He's never disappointed. He is ever hopeful for your tomorrow.

Be done pretending. Be done striving. Be done with your religion. Be done with believing everyone is dispensable. Be done waiting for the gift of nobility to hit you like a Damascus Road encounter. For God gave us free will; He's waiting for you to choose it.

But you're breathing deeper, you're loving harder, you're unstoppable now, you're seeing clearly now, you're fighting the good fight in the way it was meant to be fought, through every noble choice. Be it subtle enough for only the angels to notice or big enough for a stadium to fill the skies with a hallelujah, you can feel Him weep over your goodness, your gentleness, your faithfulness, your joy, your love, your self-control as you make more steps closer to how He made you in His image.

Man alive, He's so proud, so besotted with you, because you caught His breath. He tells everyone about you. He shouts your name from the rooftops. He sees you coming along the horizon and is desperate to embrace you. He's that's beautiful. He's that sensational. He's that matchless.

Don't, in your own self-questioning, discount His truth. The truth that shows what you hold at your own fingertips: the perseverance of Helen Roseveare, the fighting courage of Father Reid, the humility of Mother Teresa, the sacrifice of Martin Luther King Jr., the faith of the fifteen-year-old African girl, the wisdom of Daniel, the compassion of Lady Diana, the courtesy of Andrew, the generosity of the boy in the crowd of five thousand, the understanding of Mr. Taylor, the sonship of the Hells Angels, the uplifting justice of Joseph, the patience of Christ, the love of Christ, the diligence of Christ, the joy of Christ, the forgiveness of Christ, the boldness of Christ, the passion of Christ.

It's in you. All of it is in you.

It is time that we as a church started echoing the true gospel, the simple, sovereign gospel. If we could only stop thinking and, therefore, acting through a shame-tinged lens. Oh, the hope we could bring back. The people we could set free. The marriages that could occur, the families that could flourish. The love that liberates above all liberties.

With this noble power we could build into ourselves first,

then to our family, then to our neighbors, to our workplace, to our churches, to our towns, to our cities, to our counties, to our nations. Just as the butterfly effect goes, so, too, does nobility spread its wings.

You are now a whistleblower to religion yet you radiate love.

My prayer for you is that through all of this, you understand how He chooses to only meet you where you are, never waiting upon where He'd wish you were. In every attempt of this catalogue of virtues, He will celebrate you for trying at all.

May your shadows heal, may your tongue speak life, may your soul yearn for His version of justice, may your actions echo your prayers, may your hurts become a romance, may you remember His eternal perspective in all walks of life. May every individual Christian rise up to become a noble army of lovers. An entity that could create a bride worth marrying, a movement that reignites the soul to inspire—a Noble Renaissance.

ACKNOWLEDGMENTS

To the team at Emanate Books, HarperCollins: Joel Kneedler, for your belief and witty banter; for your original thoughts on topics as old as the gospels. To Larry Sparks for introducing me to Joel. Janene MacIvor, to learn from you has been such a gift, thank you for your gentleness, for your ability to hold my voice whilst ensuring I don't say "whilst" too often. You have been a great teacher and encourager. Kristen Golden, for showing me the magical sights of Nashville and for your efforts in getting this book marketed to the right people, at the right time. Timothy Paulson, for your kindness to take this book on. Joey Paul, *that* phone call could not have come at a more pertinent moment. Thank you for the kind tears and your heart to champion these words.

My travel assistant and most brilliant researcher Beth Regattieri: From research and permission citations to sleeping in log cabins with spiders and no loo just to be by my side, you were an integral part of this journey and your support has beautifully melted my heart. Thank you for your excellence and friendship.

My personal assistant Lila Richardson: Where would I be

without you and your giggles? The words I shared with you on the steps of my house, the tears of thanks and honor will never feel enough for all you do for me. My additional team help over that year of writing: Callie Allen, Gabi Gonzalez, Adam Clifford.

The Noble Army: My intercessors who poured and keep pouring into the intention of nobility. Your prayers marked an impactful note on my heart and therefore on these words. Cindy (and Justin) Butow, Elkin Antoniou, Helen Walton, Jonna Shuster, Kelsey King, Kimberly Johnson, Lindsey Reiman, Lisa (and David) Monroe, Markus Kirwald, Jared Martin, Tinasha LaRaye, Alex Hutton, Mary Webb, Jodi Hannah, Bethel Intercessors.

Additional thanks for love and devotion over this project and beyond: Zach and Hannah Canon, Scott Fontenot, Laila Elk, Father Hanz, Shelby King, Nat Mayer, Mike Meashiro, Deb Miller and Cheena, Michael Braverman, Ken and Beth Fish, Jake and Katie Veach, Laura Rae Anderson, John Ramirez, Erica Greve, Lindsey Reiman, Clare and Pete Mattis, Rebecca Couper, Joel Power, my brother—Brian Harper and the Harper family in New York. The BLN Pastors that have blessed my last year.

Teresa Archer: Since *Darling* magazine you have been a gift to me. Thank you for your editorial brilliance and divine wisdom in all matters of the heart.

Nathan Madden: You started as a giggle, but you've become so much more. Thank you for bringing not just your joy, but your tenderness and emotional brilliance to my life.

UK THANKS:

Lord George Carey: For your guidance on this subject and for allowing me into the throne room at Westminster Palace. Our chats and time together were a treasure trove for me in this project.

Robert Van De Weyer: Over the years I have listened to your stories, over the years they have given me great revelation. Thank you for letting me share some of them here. You are a gift to me and my family.

Malcolm Down: Had it not been for you and your findings of my work, I would not be here writing book three. You were the first publisher to believe in me and have been a continued friend since *The Virgin Monologues*. Whether it's drives to the airports or honest chats about love, I will always be grateful for your input and wisdom.

UK Friends: Helen Marvel, Margaret Wood, David Britton, Andy and Charlie Calton-Watson, Rachel Wood and Matt Sanderson, Kim and Dave Conlon. Special tribute to Jane and Doug Henderson for your love and steadfastness from my teenage years.

My Cousins: Ian and Alison James, Clare and Dick Saunders, Kate and Robert Saunders, Will and Emma James, Jane and Jim Dempsey. I love you dearly and am so thankful to walk this life with you.

Bobby and Elkin: Remember that day we went through two hundred names for this book? To my creative soldiers and wildlings, life with you on the same street is a dream come true. Thank you for your effervescent passion.

For the ones who truly do change the world in both their philanthropic and solution orientated mindsets—the true peacemakers—Maggie, Joe, and Sharon Ritchie. Thank you for being such a substance to learn from, a family to tuck under the wing of, the space for which the finest writers only wish they could write in the Round Room.

The Truth-Tellers: Maggie Ritchie, Lori and James Burke,

Toni and Paul Matta for your continual reference on character that grew these pages to be thicker in wisdom. Dann Farrelly, Rich Schmidt and Kris Vallotton. Gabe Valenzuela: For having the conversations so few are willing to have. Pappa Rex: For your daily encouragement. Dave Harvey: Your covering and positivity has been transformative, thank you!

Krystal Gowan and my goddaughter Quinn: You fought for me through so many seasons and taught me what strength and endurance with Him really looks like.

Dawn O'Porter and Chris O'Dowd: For your alternative title suggestions. And for all the cheese.

Amanda Cook: From Redding to Nashville, Hawaii to England, Paris to our home in Los Angeles, you have been the ever constant, my giggler from the west to the east. My guts may sue you one day for all the laughter they had to endure. You are the heights of hilarity and the depths of emotional expression. The wordsmith on the piano and the maker of my morning coffee. Thank you for creating this beautiful life with me in friendship. Hello to a new era. Hello to our Lord, our Jesus.

Richard and Kathleen Downs: Your dreams of what I could do became tangible, became podcasts, became books, became dinnertime stories. Your hospitality and unconditional love is a life jacket in the deep ocean of pastoring, thank you for being the lighthouse and being such loyal friends.

Kim and Bob Johnson: The warriors who taught me what it could look like to be fearless, to fight for what He grieves over, to remember the lost, the outcast, the poor. You were an inspiration for this book, and your friendship in all its beautiful colors has been a privilege.

Bill Johnson: I may never have written a third book if it hadn't been for your kind nudges. Thank you for personifying the noble character so much that I could believe it was accessible for all of us. Your friendship, marriage to Beni, and fruitful family have been some of the finest gifts to have ever walked into my life. Any attempts of gratitude will never feel enough, but I will keep trying. As I wrote to you once before, your kindness is as perennial as the grass and, oh, the mountains it has moved in not just me, but in generations.

May Lloyd: Mrs Tiggywinkles, my mother, my most steadfast soul, your every-day love, the way you hold a room captivated with your peace, your brilliant mind, and your sensational humor, from your newspaper clippings to your emails that should be published, thank you for reminding me of the important elements, for introducing me to the greatest entity anyone could introduce mc to—Jesus and His love for this beautiful world.

NOTES

Chapter 1: Barefoot in the Rain

1. A. W. Tozer and H. Verploegh, *The Set of the Sail* (Chicago, IL: Moody Publishers, 2007), 178.
2. Michael Hart, *The 100: A Ranking of the Most Influential Persons in History* (New York: Citadel, 1978, 1992), 100.
3. Hart, *The 100*, 20.
4. Hart, *The 100*, 20.
5. Gordon Tredgold, "29 Surprising Facts That Explain Why Millennials See the World Differently," *Inc.*, May 2, 2016, https://www.inc.com/gordon-tredgold/29-surprising-facts -about-millennials-and-what-motivates-them.html.
6. Chris Smith, dir., *Frye* (2019, Library Films, Via Studios, and Jerry Media, distributed by Netflix).

Chapter 2: Pass the Milk

1. *Thatcher: A Very British Executive*, producer: Steve Condie, director: James House (2019, June 7). Retrieved January 13, 2020, https://www.bbc.co.uk/programmes/m0005br9.

Chapter 3: Annus Horribilis

1. HRH Queen Elizabeth, "A Speech by the Queen on the 40th Anniversary of Her Succession," published November 24, 1992, Royal.uk, https://www.royal.uk/annus-horribilis-speech.
2. Queen Elizabeth, "A Speech by the Queen."
3. Galatians 5:22–23: "But the fruit of the Spirit is love, joy, peace, long-suffering, kindness, gentleness, self-control."
4. H. Roseveare, *Living Faith* (Great Britain: Christian Focus Pub, 2007). Used by permission.

Chapter 4: Emperors of Truth

1. Channel 4 TV program on Online Dating 2012.
2. From a draft television address, April 1955. Published in Nathan and Norden, *Einstein on Peace*, 640. AEA 60-003 With permission: Hebrew University of Jerusalem.

Chapter 5: "From Now On, Only the Pilot Can Fly the Plane"

1. Joel Stein, "Millennials: The Me Me Me Generation," *Time*, May 20, 2013, https://time.com/247/millennials-the-me-me-me-generation/.
2. Richard Alleyne, "Young Adults Believe in the Age of Entitlement, Claim Researchers," *Telegraph*, May 24, 2010, https://www.telegraph.co.uk/news/uknews/7760687/Young-adults-believe-in-the-age-of-entitlement-claim-researchers.html.
3. Danielle Fowler, "Millennials Admit They're 'Scared' to Answer the Doorbell in Hilarious Twitter Thread," Yahoo Style UK, June 4, 2019, https://news.yahoo.com/millennials-answer-doorbell-163253984.html.
4. William Barclay, *The Mind of Jesus* (New York: HarperCollins, 1976), 21.
5. Oscar speech February 10, 2020.

Chapter 6: Die Tryin'

1. The feeding of the five thousand is described in Matthew 14, Mark 6, Luke 9, and John 6.
2. *Noble* can also be translated here as *honorable*.

Chapter 7: The Bitter Taste of Vanilla

1. Vance Christie, *Women of Faith and Courage* (Christian Focus Publications, 2011), 177.
2. Michael Apted, dir., *Amazing Grace* (2006, Bristol Bay Productions).

Chapter 8: Southern White-Faced Owl

1. Robert Sternberg, "Speculation on the Role of Successful Intelligence in Solving Contemporary World Problems," *Journal of Intelligence* 6:1 (March 2018), 4.
2. Amy Morin, "Science Explains the Link Between Self-Compassion and Success," *Forbes*, October 1, 2015, https://www .forbes.com/sites/amymorin/2015/10/01/science-explains-the -link-between-self-compassion-and-success/.
3. The most recent evidence suggests that this trend may now be slowing. It may even be reversing, meaning that we have already passed the summit of human intellectual potential. David Robson, "Has Humanity Reached 'Peak Intelligence?'" BBC Future, July 10, 2019, http://www.bbc.com/future/article /20190709-has-humanity-reached-peak-intelligence.

Chapter 9: Sunt Lacrimae Rerum

1. T. Newman, "Anxiety in the West: Is It on the Rise?" September 5, 2018, retrieved January 13, 2020, *Medical News Today*, https:// www.medicalnewstoday.com/articles/322877.php#4.
2. A. Kleinman (2013, May 4). "Porn Sites Get More Visitors Each Month Than Netflix, Amazon and Twitter Combined," HuffPost Canada, May 4, 2013, retrieved January 13, 2020, https://www.huffpost.com/entry/internet-porn-stats_n_3187682.

3. C. S. Lewis, *The Problem with Pain* (London: HarperCollins, 2012).

Chapter 10: Angels of Mercy

1. Jerrod Brown, "Father-Absent Homes: Implications for Criminal Justice and Mental Health Professionals," Minnesota Psychological Association, https://www.mnpsych.org/index.php%3Foption%3Dcom_dailyplanetblog%26view%3Dentry%26category%3Dindustry%2520news%26id%3D54.

2. Jack Frost, *Experiencing Father's Embrace* (Destiny Image, 2006).

ABOUT THE AUTHOR

C arrie Lloyd is a UK journalist and author of *The Virgin Monologues* and *Prude*. As an atheist turned Christian, she is now a pastor in California and works between England and her residence in Hollywood. Her *Carrie On* podcast is a discussion about life, relationships, choices, and nobility. She is an activist against sex-trafficking and an advocate for orphan welfare.

www.carrielloyd.live